Making Whoopee

ALSO BY EVAN MORRIS

The Word Detective
The Book Lover's Guide to the Internet

Making Whoopee

Words of Love
for Lovers of Words

by Evan Morris

Algonquin Books
of Chapel Hill

2004

Published by

Algonquin Books of Chapel Hill

Post Office Box 2225

Chapel Hill, North Carolina 27515-2225

a division of

Workman Publishing

708 Broadway

New York, New York 10003

Printed in the United States of America.

Published simultaneously in Canada

by Thomas Allen & Son Limited.

Design by Anne Winslow.

Library of Congress Cataloging-in-Publication Data

Morris, Evan.

    Making whoopee : words of love for lovers of words / by Evan Morris.—1st ed.

      p. cm.

    Includes bibliographical references.

    ISBN 1-56512-350-6

    1. English language—Terms and phrases.   2. English language—Etymology.

    3. Love—Terminology. I. Title.

PE1583.M67 2004

  422'.03—dc22   2003060151

10 9 8 7 6 5 4 3 2 1

First Edition

For Kathy, who defines love for me.

ACKNOWLEDGMENTS

Thanks to my wife, Kathy Wollard, for coming up with the idea for this book and for her suggestions, assistance, and good advice throughout its writing. Thanks also to my family, friends, and all my readers for their encouragement and support; to my agent, Janis Donnaud, for her hard work and valuable guidance; to my editor, Amy Gash, for the perceptive suggestions and skillful editing that made this book blossom; to my copy editor, Rachel Careau, for her awesome attention to detail, and to all the folks at Algonquin for shepherding this book into print.

INTRODUCTION

Love is a talkative passion.
—Bishop Thomas Wilson

That's putting it mildly. Lovers, it would seem, love to talk about love as much as they love to love. More words have been spoken and written about love than about any other part of our lives. From Shakespeare's sonnets to the great operas to the classic novels, love—love sought, love lost, or love found—has been the name of the game. Love not only makes the world go round, but it fills our libraries, bookstores, and magazine stands, our motion pictures and television shows, not to mention the supermarket tabloids.

Like all grand passions, love has its own vocabulary. A lover may say, "Words fail me," but that certainly hasn't stopped people from trying to capture the mystery of love in words. In fact, for something so notoriously hard to define, love has spawned a remarkable collection of words and phrases that we use to express, explain, describe, and define love to one another. Lovers may *flirt, date, neck, cuddle,* and *fondle* each other, and still they have only begun to speak the special language of love.

The language of love is ancient, and many of the words we use today have their roots in the ancient world. This makes perfect sense, of course, since if there hadn't been love and romance at the dawn of time, the descendants of those primordial lovers wouldn't be reading this book today and my publisher would be very upset.

Many of our modern "love words" hark back to Greece and Rome, proving that some things, especially when it comes to matters of the heart, never change. Words such as *erotic, infatuation, amorous,* and *adore* are all rooted in Greek or Latin, as are some evoking the downside of love, such as *divorce* and *alimony.* The epic love affairs of gods and goddesses of Greek and Roman mythology have proved far more durable in our language than they were in the myths themselves—witness such contemporary words as *aphrodisiac, Adonis, venereal,* and *Cupid.*

But every generation prefers to believe that it invented, or at least improved, romance, love, and especially sex, and every crop of new lovers brings at least a few new words of slang. Like all slang, the popular terminology of love and sex at any given moment functions to separate the in-group from the outcasts, in this case the knowing young from the hopelessly lame old. Your niece rolls her eyes when you use the term *necking* for the same reason you shuddered when your grandmother waxed nostalgic over *spooning.* But someday, in the not distant future, all that is now in will be out, and the current *hit on* (meaning "proposition") will sound every bit as dated as the mid-twentieth century *make a pass.*

Furthermore, until someone invents a category of human romantic behavior that is truly novel, the vernacular of love will always fall into the same broad categories. The name may have changed, but the practice called *courting* looked a lot like *spooning,* which begot *dating,* went a bit vague with *seeing* ("Are you still seeing Freddie?"), and now founders in the mechanical *hooking up,* meaning anything from "going steady" to "having a one-night stand." Likewise *paramour, lover, boyfriend/girlfriend,* and *steady* all describe the same general kind of relationship, although the awkward modern invention *significant other* sounds like it was born on a census form.

Occasionally, however, the process of linguistic invention seems to stall, and we are treated to the sound of fourteenth-century words coming from the mouths of nineteen-year-olds. In particular, and perhaps significantly, most words having to do with the institution of marriage have not changed in hundreds of years. While the lingo of the carefree single life changes almost annually, no one in the last few centuries seems to have come up with snappy alternatives to *engagement, fiancé/fiancée, bride, groom,* or even *honeymoon.* There must be something about those somber vows that sobers up even the flippest slang slinger.

One of the advantages of English's being a large language drawn from many sources is the amount of elbow room it gives its users to develop subtle differences of meaning for words and expressions that are, theoretically, nearly synonymous.

Dear, darling, and *honey* are all popular endearments, but "Yes, dear" will never carry the emotional oomph of "Yes, darling." To suffer from a *crush* on someone is less painful (not to mention less time-consuming) than *to pine* for the same person. *Bliss* isn't quite the same as *ecstasy,* although it may last longer. And no one who has weathered the storms of love would miss the distinction between *boyfriend* and *friend* or *to love* and *to be in love.*

Many words and phrases of love have changed their meanings dramatically over the centuries, tracing a tangled trajectory of mutation that leaves their modern meanings miles from their origin. *Lewd,* in the twelfth century, simply meant "not a member of the clergy," a far cry from its modern connotation of "sexually suggestive." And centuries before *philanderer* came to mean "a man who is an adulterer," it meant just "one who loves mankind."

Predicting the future is always a risky (and usually a futile) endeavor, and never more so than in the field of popular speech. Given the trend toward apathetic vagueness in slang lately ("So, like, she goes, 'Whatever'"), one might expect more inventions along the lines of the impersonal *hook up.* The volatility and fickleness of popular culture today probably guarantee that we won't see the likes of the literary *Lothario, Casanova,* or even *Romeo* emerging from TV sitcoms or ephemeral boy bands. And while computer jargon has given us the useful *spam, reboot,* and even the semisocial *F2F* (*face-to-face,* that is, in real life), the Internet's main contribution to the language of love and sex may have been to popularize *cybersex* and to boost the form *porn* over the older *porno.* Then again, perhaps we'll soon see a new category of relationship based on cell phones and text messaging ("She's been texting him for six months, but all the time he was call-waiting her with Sherri, so she erased him"). Or perhaps a fad for all things medieval will catch on and we'll be back speaking of *swains, maidens,* and *betrothals* (although that's probably just wishful thinking on my part). But whatever the future brings, the language of love and romance will endure, for as long as birds do it and bees do it, we'll have to have a name for it.

got to date the goddess of love, so Adonis gave Persephone the big brush-off. Persephone, understandably annoyed, then did what any jealous lover–foster mother–goddess would: she picked up the phone and dropped a dime on the lovebirds to Ares, Aphrodite's longtime significant other. Ares, angry as a wild boar, then took the form of a real wild boar, tracked Adonis down, and gored him to death. The moral of this story appears to be, You may think you're blessed by the gods, but watch out for the disgruntled boyfriend.

Adultery

Although adultery is usually committed by people beyond the age of majority, *adultery* has nothing to do with the word *adult. Adult,* meaning "having reached maturity," comes from the Latin *adultus,* past participle of the verb *adolescere,* meaning "to grow up" (and the source of our *adolescence*). Attaining adulthood is generally considered a good thing.

Adultery, as any adult can tell you, is a different kettle of fish. The Latin root of *adultery* says it all: *adulterare,* meaning "to corrupt," "to spoil," or "to make foul." In English since around 1415, *adultery* has meant "the act of voluntary sexual intercourse between

ADULTERY meaning to corrupt or spoil something else (usually applied to food) carries heavier legal penalties in Western societies than does sexual adultery.

Adonis

An *Adonis* is an extremely attractive young man of the sort also sometimes referred to breathlessly by persons of the female persuasion as a *Greek god*. Men who resent such gushing can take comfort in the fact that the original Adonis was not a god at all but rather, as the Greek gods themselves put it, a "mere mortal." And Adonis, chiseled chin and buff pecs notwithstanding, did not come to a good end.

Adonis did have a remarkable run while it lasted. As an infant, he was adopted by none other than Aphrodite, the goddess of love. But since Adonis was still a baby and goddesses of love have better things to do than change Pampers and dispense strained beets, Aphrodite left Adonis in the care of Persephone, queen of the underworld, for a few years.

When Aphrodite returned years later to pick Adonis up, she made two discoveries, one good, one not so good. First of all, Adonis had grown into a major hunk, which set Aphrodite's heart a-thumpin' despite the fact that she was his quasi stepmother. But the bad news was that Persephone had fallen in love with Adonis herself and had no plans to give him up to Aphrodite. Much acrimony ensued until Zeus, head honcho of the gods, stepped in to mediate.

Zeus devised a time-sharing agreement whereby Aphrodite and Persephone would each get, well, let's call it *custody* of Adonis for six months out of the year. But Aphrodite pretty quickly convinced Adonis that it wasn't every day a mere mortal a married person and another to whom he or she is not married." (Strictly speaking, if the other person is married as well, such activity constitutes *double adultery*.)

Historically, adultery has been condemned as corrupting or spoiling the marriage vows, although the practice has never been as rare nor its consequences as dire as some folks would like. Ironically, a derivative sense of *adultery* meaning to corrupt or spoil something else (usually applied to food) carries heavier legal penalties in Western societies than does sexual adultery. The point is that it's OK to fool around as long as you don't water down the ketchup.

Alimony

It may or may not be true that two can live as cheaply as one. But it is beyond dispute that two, once no longer together, often cannot live without vigorously wrestling over the joint checking account. Back in the days before prenuptial agreements, society intervened in such disputes and almost always decreed that upon divorce the husband had to make regular payments of *alimony* to his former wife (or former wives, in the case of slow learners). The function of alimony (as can be deduced from the term's origin

Thanks to the coinage of PALIMONY and the eternal inventiveness of lawyers, we can now presumably look forward to court cases seeking FLIRT-IMONY, DATE-IMONY, and perhaps even LONGING-GLANCE-IMONY.

in the Latin *alere,* meaning "to nourish") was to ensure that the wife had not jumped from the frying pan of a bad marriage into the fire of penury. In rare cases, mostly in Hollywood, an underachieving husband was awarded alimony from his wealthier wife.

After liberalized social expectations made formal marriage more or less optional in the late twentieth century, couples who had cohabited for years or even decades parted without a legal claim on each other's wealth. Such a litigation vacuum greatly annoyed the legal community, again especially in Hollywood. Thus in the late 1970s the first court actions were brought seeking *palimony,* wherein a celebrity was held to financial account for his or her extended dalliance with a noncelebrity "pal." The suffix *mony* didn't really mean anything in the case of *alimony,* but thanks to the coinage of *palimony* and the eternal inventiveness of lawyers, we can now presumably look forward to court cases seeking *flirt-imony, date-imony,* and perhaps even *longing-glance-imony.*

Allure

Allure is, etymologically speaking, just bait. All the cologne, sports cars, health-club memberships, little black dresses, expensive suits, liposuction, jewelry, tanning salons, and Italian shoes, not to mention the Hair Club for Men—all those doodads and enhancements, the entire accessory kit of romance, is really nothing more than a worm on the hook of love. Furthermore, *allure* originally had nothing to do with attracting other humans. The Old French *loirre* was a device—a bunch of feathers swung on a string—used in falconry to call the bird back to the falconer. The term was imported into English as *lure* in the fifteenth century and soon took on the more general sense of "something that entices or tempts." By about 1700, *lure* was being used in its modern sense of "bait" in fishing and hunting.

Meanwhile, the related Old French verb *alurer,* meaning "to attract or captivate," had become the English *allurer,* which by 1612 was being used to mean "to fascinate, charm, or tempt." The thing used as bait was originally known as an *allurement,* but by the mid–sixteenth century the shorter modern noun form *allure* was common.

Today, *allure* can mean the attraction exerted by nearly anything over anyone, but the most common usage is in the sense of "sexual temptation." And when one of the most successful women's magazines on the market today is called *Allure,* we can be fairly certain they're not selling tips on catching trout.

Animal Magnetism

No, we're not talking about the strange force that allows flies to walk on the ceiling. *Animal magnetism* is the strange force that allows, however briefly, Rhodes Scholars to marry professional wrestlers. The

ANIMAL MAGNETISM is the strange force that allows, however briefly, Rhodes Scholars to marry professional wrestlers.

afflicted parties invariably ascribe their feelings to "love at first sight" or "fate," but the nineteenth century had its own explanation: animal magnetism or mesmerization.

Mesmerize is an eponym, a word formed from the name of a person or place. In the case of *mesmerize,* the person was a German physician named Franz Anton Mesmer (1734–1815), who managed in the course of his long career to be spectacularly wrong about almost everything.

Although Dr. Mesmer graduated from a prestigious medical school in Vienna, he was a pretty weird dude right from the get-go. In his doctoral thesis, Mesmer proposed the existence of a mysterious universal force, which he would later dub *animal magnetism,* that permeated and governed all living things. Mesmer believed that he could manipulate this force and cure his patients simply by stroking them with magnets. Not surprisingly, Mesmer was adjudged a quack and run out of Vienna, but he landed in Paris, where he soon became a favorite of Marie-Antoinette and her court. Fashionable Parisians flocked to Mesmer's group sessions, where patients would hold hands and dip their feet in tubs of "magnetized" water while Mesmer pranced around them, speaking softly and waving a magic wand. Many of his patients reported miraculous cures.

What Mesmer had actually done, without realizing it, was to hypnotize his patients into thinking they were cured, which in many cases worked because they weren't really very sick to begin with. Mesmer was eventually discredited by a scientific commission that included Benjamin Franklin, but his *mesmerizing* was immortalized as a synonym for "hypnotizing," and *animal magnetism* is still heard today as an explanation for unlikely romantic pairings.

Aphrodisiac

Power is the great aphrodisiac.
—Henry Kissinger

Now you tell us, Henry. For thousands of years, human beings who found their love life lukewarm have searched for a substance that would supercharge the libido. From Spanish fly (actually a powder made from dried beetles) to Viagra, the path to love (or at least lust) has been charted through pills, potions, and spells. It's a bit depressing to think attractiveness might simply reside in one's résumé.

Aphrodite, the Greek goddess of love, made a career of living up to her title. Although Zeus gave her in marriage to Hephaestus, Aphrodite's extracurricular paramours included fellow divinities Hermes, Ares, Dionysus, and even Zeus himself, not to mention a few

> While Aphrodite is remembered with APHRODISIAC, poor Venus is linguistically noted for inspiring the term VENEREAL DISEASE.

regular guys on rainy afternoons. As one might expect, *aphrodisiac* came to mean "pertaining to sexual desire" as well as "a drug or preparation inducing sexual desire" in English.

Many Greek gods were later adopted by the Romans, and Aphrodite's Roman equivalent was Venus. Unfortunately, Venus could have used a good public relations agent. While Aphrodite is remembered with *aphrodisiac,* poor Venus is linguistically noted for inspiring *venereal,* which, although it technically means "associated with sexual desire," is most commonly encountered in the phrase *venereal disease.*

Ardor

There's *ardor* and then there's real *romantic ardor.* Although *ardor* is used today as a simple synonym for "enthusiasm," when the word first appeared in English in the fourteenth century it meant "overwhelming passion," "burning desire," or "vehemence." English borrowed *ardor* from the Old French *ardour,* which was drawn from the Latin *ardere,* meaning "to burn."

English borrowed ARDOR from the Old French ARDOUR, which was drawn from the Latin ARDERE, meaning "to burn."

Bachelor

Still more evidence that the English language is not fair. A *bachelor* is a man who is not married, a state that would seem to encompass enough members of both sexes that there should be an equivalent one-word term for a woman who is not married. Yet there is not: an unmarried woman is called simply *an unmarried woman.* And that's not the end of it. A woman upon marriage becomes a *wife;* a man, a *husband.* If one or the other expires while still married, the survivor becomes a *widow* or *widower,* respectively. But should divorce intervene, the woman becomes a *divorcée,* while the man (though technically a *divorcé*) simply goes back to being called a *bachelor.* And while it's true that the term *divorcée* is rarely heard these days, the only real alternative is the awkward *single woman.* Occasional inventions such as *bachelor girl* or the dreadful *bachelorette* have remained mercifully unpopular.

Furthermore, it's not as though *bachelor* even meant "unmarried man" when we borrowed it from the Old French *bacheler* in the thirteenth century. The first bachelors were apprentice knights, relegated to polishing the head honcho's armor and grooming his horse. The next notable sense of *bachelor* to develop was "one who has achieved the first degree at a university," as opposed to the more advanced *master of arts* (both of which terms are still in use). Since most university bachelors were young men, not yet married, by the late fourteenth century *bachelor* had taken on its modern meaning of "unmarried man."

If there is any justice to be found in the *bachelor/ whatchamacallit* conundrum, it may lie in one possible source of the word *bachelor* itself. Many experts believe that the ultimate root of *bachelor* is the Vulgar Latin *baccalaris,* which meant "farmhand" and was from the Latin *vacca,* meaning "cow."

Betroth

Looking for a linguistic time machine? Try getting married. No matter how many new words and phrases we invent to describe love and romance, as soon as someone pops The Question, we're back in the vernacular of the fourteenth century. The effect can be disconcerting: for chronological vertigo, there aren't many sentences that can match newspaper announcements, not uncommon today, such as "The Web designer and the performance artist were betrothed last month."

To betroth means "to promise to marry," and *betrothed* means "engaged to be married." The noun *troth,* though it sounds obscurely medieval, is simply another form of the word *truth,* and when *troth* first appeared in English in the twelfth century, it meant "good faith," "loyalty," or "honesty." One's troth was one's word, a solemn promise to do something. *To betroth* was to make and be bound by a promise, specifically a promise to marry. As of about 1300, *to betroth* was what a man did in pledging to marry a woman, but by the sixteenth century the term was applied as well to a woman promising to marry a man.

One of the weirder archaic locutions occasionally heard in

the vicinity of engagement parties is *to plight one's troth,* meaning "to get engaged." Although we know *plight* today as a noun meaning "dire predicament" (a sense reflecting its origin in the Old English *pliht,* meaning "danger")," *plight one's troth* is not a warning about marriage per se. A later sense of *plight* as a verb was "to pledge on pain of danger or forfeiture," meaning that if you plight your troth and then back out, bad things will happen. But your future father-in-law could have told you that.

Billet-Doux

A *billet-doux* is a little love note, and the term comes directly from the French for "sweet note." We've been writing *billets-doux* (the plural form) in English since the seventeenth century.

A proper billet-doux is inscribed on fine paper and may, if written by a woman, be lightly scented with perfume to amplify its impact. Writing style is very important to the success of the billet-doux. When done correctly, the billet-doux conveys deep yearning with a lightness of touch that beckons the beloved to cast worldly cares and social conventions aside and join the writer in a dance through the dreamy spring meadows of love.

An E-mail reading "Meet me at Starbucks" is not a billet-doux and should, along with its sender, be ignored.

> An E-mail reading "Meet me at Starbucks" is not a billet-doux and should, along with its sender, be ignored.

Bimbo

Ain't who? The odd thing about Raymond Chandler's use of *bimbo* in that quotation is that the author is clearly referring to a man, yet *bimbo* today is exclusively used to mean "an attractive but not very bright young woman." But our modern sense of *bimbo* was not the original meaning. When *bimbo,* which is a shortened form of *bambino,* Italian for "child" or "baby," first appeared in English around 1919, it originally meant a young person of either gender and, in fact, was most often applied to men. When a gangster spoke of a *bimbo* in the 1920s, chances were that he was referring to the sort of dim-witted street-corner thug we might today call a *wise-guy wanna-be.*

When a gangster spoke of a BIMBO in the 1920s, chances were that he was referring to the sort of dim-witted street-corner thug we might today call a WISE-GUY WANNA-BE.

The shift of gender in the popular use of *bimbo* to mean a young woman who trades on her appearance in lieu of talent or intellect remains a mystery, although we do know that it began sometime in the late 1920s and that the transformation of *bimbo* from he to she was complete by the 1940s.

Blind Date

In describing your blind date, I would say she has a wonderful personality.

—*Chicago Tribune*

I t is, given that quotation, not surprising that the earliest citation for *kiss of death* in the *Oxford English Dictionary* comes from the very next year, 1948. *Wonderful personality* is the classic kiss of death when it comes to blind dates. People bracing themselves to go on blind dates don't want to hear that their date-to-be has a wonderful personality. They want to hear the words *stunning* or *knockout* or, from the feminine viewpoint, the elusive *debonair hunk.*

A *blind date* is a date, usually arranged by a third party, between two people who have not previously met. Although people who are literally sightless no doubt also go on blind dates, the use of *blind* in this context is figurative, meaning "without direct observation or foreknowledge," much

What such adventures were called before BLIND DATE first appeared around 1925 is uncertain, but the simple and direct BAD IDEA is one possibility.

as an pilot might make a "blind approach" to an unfamiliar landing strip or consumers might be subjected to a "blind taste test" of powdered coffee brands. What such adventures were called before *blind date* first appeared around 1925 is uncertain, but the simple and direct *bad idea* is one possibility.

Bliss

The key to bliss, wedded or otherwise, can be found in six little words: *Don't let it get to you.* The origin of the word *bliss* itself, meaning "joy," "happiness," or "deep contentment," bears this out. The root of *bliss* is the ancient Germanic *blithiz,* "kind, cheerful, gentle," which entered Old English as *blithis,* in the sense of "happiness," and became our modern bliss in the sixteenth century. But along the way, *blithis* spawned another common English word: *blithe,* defined as "glad," "cheerful," "lighthearted," or "carefree." The blithe soul is not troubled by a partner's peccadilloes or personal quirks and does not go ballistic over the small stuff, be it underwear on the bathroom floor or beer nuts in the bedsheets. Blithe people probably live longer and have a better shot at living those years in bliss.

Boyfriend

> Yes! Yes! Say it! He vas my BOYFRIEND!
>
> —*Young Frankenstein*

Frau Blucher had it right. A *boyfriend* is more than just a friend who is a boy, although both *boy* and *friend* are interesting words in their own right. Back in the thirteenth century, *boy* (from the Old French *embuier,* meaning "fetter" or "restriction") originally meant "male servant." The more general sense of "young man" developed in the fourteenth century. *Friend* harks back to a very old Germanic root meaning "love," and since it first appeared in Old English, a *friend* has been "one attached to another by affection and esteem."

Boyfriend came into general use (initially as *boy-friend*) in the late nineteenth century, and from the outset *boyfriend* was generally understood to be a euphemism for "lover," as it remains today. *Boyfriend* is an equal-opportunity term and can be used to refer to both straight and gay relationships.

Bride

Given that the English language is constantly changing and evolving, adding new words and discarding those made suddenly obsolete, the history of *bride* is notable for the word's near-total lack of evolution over the past millennium. The word *bride* has meant "woman about to be married or just married" ever since it was first borrowed into Old English (as *bryd*) from Germanic languages back around A.D. 1000. True, the spellings of *bride* at various times have included such (to our eyes) odd early forms as *brede, brude, brid, bruyd,* and *bryde,* but even our modern spelling of *bride* has been standard since the fourteenth century. Unfortunately, *bride* is so old a word, and has so many relatives in other languages, that its origin is a bit obscure. Most likely its earliest antecedents meant "woman about to be

Mom, Dad, Meet My ... My ...

For as long as there have been parents and snoopy relatives, the question of what to call the person one is currently "seeing" has made for awkward introductions. Here is a guide to a few of the popular choices.

Boyfriend/Girlfriend: The no-risk fallback, implying nothing more than sharing an occasional ice-cream soda. Works well with all relatives but sounds silly if you're over thirty.

Paramour: From the Middle French *par amour,* meaning "by or through love." Implies grand, if transient, passion. Perhaps a bit risqué for introductions to Mom and Dad, but works well at dinner parties.

Lover: Admirably direct, but emphasizes the sexual aspect of your relationship and will cause cringing in older relatives.

Consort: Dates back to the fifteenth century and originally meant simply "a partner or friend," later "husband or wife." Usually used in reference to the spouse of a monarch (as Prince Albert was called Queen Victoria's *consort*). Most people have only a vague idea of what it means and will be afraid to ask, so go for it.

Fiancé/Fiancée: From the French *fiancer,* "to betroth." Works well with landlords and motel clerks but may cause later complications with relatives (unless you really *are* engaged).

Main Squeeze: Cute 1940s term for one's girlfriend, coyly implying that there are other, secondary paramours on the side. OK as a joke, but repeated use may degrade your relationship.

Steady: Musty 1950s term drawn from *going steady,* that is, exclusively dating one person. Works well with grandparents, but conjures up Dick Clark for everyone else.

Old Lady/Old Man: Avoid unless you own a motorcycle. A *big* motorcycle.

Significant Other: A noble but doomed attempt, dating back to the 1970s, to sidestep the "Are you guys married?" question entirely. OK for use on party invitations (where it is sometimes mercifully abbreviated *S.O.*), but anyone who can say *significant other* aloud with a straight face probably owns a cat named Che and should be avoided.

Partner/Domestic Partner: As a definition in legislation and insurance coverage, a valuable invention. As a social introduction, *domestic partner* is too weirdly clinical, but *partner* is acceptable, as long as you're prepared to be asked what business the two of you own.

Companion: *Companion* is a little twitchy but OK to use once per occasion. Repeated use will make you sound like members of a cult.

Very Good Friend/Special Friend: Creepy circumlocutions that manage to mix *Sesame Street*–cute with tabloid smarminess. Best to go with a simple *my friend* and let everyone speculate after you've left the room.

married." But there is some evidence that a precursor of *bride* actually meant "daughter-in-law," and was based on an old Germanic root word meaning "to cook," cooking having been the duty of the daughter-in-law in primitive Germanic families.

The adjective *bridal,* incidentally, did not originally mean "pertaining to a bride or wedding," as it does today. The *bride-ale* was the wedding feast (Old English *brydealu*), so called on account of the vast quantities of ale served.

Carnal

Although *carnal knowledge* is an established euphemism for "sexual intimacy" these days, *carnal* originally had a much broader meaning than just "lustful."

In the beginning was *carnalis,* Latin for "of the flesh," derived from *caro,* "flesh" or "meat," and also the root of *carnivore, carnage,* and even *carnival,* originally a festival (literally, "removal of meat") preceding the meatless observation of Lent.

When CARNAL first appeared in English in the fifteenth century, it was as the opposite of "heavenly" or "spiritual" —one's carnal or worldly possessions, one's horse, house, or business, as compared to the state of one's soul.

When *carnal* first appeared in English in the fifteenth century, it was as the opposite of "heavenly" or "spiritual"—one's carnal or worldly possessions, one's horse, house, or business, as compared to the state of one's soul. In another sense, *carnal* was used to signify the human body and all its sensations and appetites—hunger, fear, greed, anger, and so forth. It was from this sense that *carnal* began to be applied more exclusively to things sexual, as it is to this day.

Carry a Torch

Thou fair-hair'd angel of the evening,
Now, whilst the sun rests on the mountains, light
Thy bright torch of love; thy radiant crown
Put on, and smile upon our evening bed!

—William Blake, "To the Evening Star"

The problem with that "bright torch of love" business is that some people, unfortunately, keep emoting right past the point when the torch burns out. Since at least 1927, *to carry the torch* (or *to carry a torch for someone*) has meant to continue to love and pine for someone long after the object of affection has left the building and any reasonable hope of amorous success has passed. By 1934, romantic ballads of lost love and broken hearts were known as *torch songs,* and female nightclub singers who made them their specialty were known as *torch singers.*

By 1934, romantic ballads of lost love and broken hearts were known as TORCH SONGS, and female nightclub singers who made them their specialty were known as TORCH SINGERS.

Just how the torch came to symbolize romantic obsession is a bit unclear, though there are several possible sources. According to legend, the Greek philosopher Diogenes of Sinope (died circa 320 B.C.) spent considerable time wandering around the countryside in broad daylight bearing either a lamp or a torch, looking for an honest man, a quest that certainly satisfies the "futility" aspect of *carry a torch*. On the other hand, Venus, the goddess of love, is often depicted bearing a torch, and the Statue of Liberty in New York Harbor is famous for her beacon of hope. Most likely, *carry a torch* simply arose from the image of a torch as an aid to searching for lost love.

Casanova

Giovanni Giacomo Casanova de Seingalt (1725–98) counted among his occupations that of soldier, journalist, philosopher, gambler, diplomat, seminarian, and spy. But he is best remembered for his memoirs, in which he detailed his thousands of amorous conquests. By modern standards, Casanova's autobiography would be considered fairly tame (although only expurgated versions were published until 1960), but the sheer monomaniacal volume of

Casanova's romantic adventures (one wonders when he got all that writing done) has made *Casanova* a popular synonym for "relentless womanizer."

Chaperon

Those crazy kids. Leave 'em alone for one minute and biology takes over, and pretty soon you've got a *situation* on your hands. At least that was the popular wisdom until relatively recently, and still is in some cultures, where a young man and a young woman spending any time alone together before marriage is considered unwise if not actually scandalous. It was to avoid such sticky situations that the tradition of the chaperon was invented.

A *chaperon* (sometimes spelled *chaperone*) is an adult, often a married or elderly woman, who accompanies an unmarried young woman on social engagements or journeys in order to safeguard her virtue and reputation.

One might suspect that the original meaning of *chaperon* was "wet blanket," and one would not be far off the mark. The Old French word *chaperon* meant "head covering" or "hood" and was rooted in the Late Latin *cappa,* meaning "hood," which is also the source of our English *cap* and *cape.* When it first appeared in

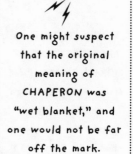

One might suspect that the original meaning of CHAPERON was "wet blanket," and one would not be far off the mark.

English in the fourteenth century, *chaperon* meant the cape or hood often worn by noblewomen. But by around 1700 *chaperon* had taken on the metaphorical meaning of "one who shelters a young woman from the world," much as a cape or hood shelters the wearer. Of course, a hood or cape may easily be discarded when it becomes inconvenient, but a chaperon, as young people have discovered for centuries, is not so easy to shake off.

Chastity

Strictly speaking (and we are speaking of chastity, after all), *chastity* simply means "moral purity," and comes directly from the Latin *castus,* meaning "pure" or "holy." But as in all matters of morals, one's chastity mileage may vary according to the exact definition in use.

When *chastity* first appeared in English in the thirteenth century, it meant "abstinence from sexual intercourse; virginity." But less than one hundred years later, *chastity* was being used to mean "purity from unlawful sexual intercourse" (*lawful* in this instance meaning "married"). This apparent contradiction was addressed by William Bauldwin in his *A Treatise of Morall Philosophie* (circa 1547), who declared that marriage constitutes a second

William Bauldwin in his A TREATISE OF MORALL PHILOSOPHIE (circa 1547) declared that marriage constitutes a second chance at CHASTITY.

chance at chastity: "The first degree of chastity is pure virginity, and the second faithfull matrimony." By the eighteenth century, *chastity* was also being used more generally to mean "moderation" or "restraint" in everything from style of dress to social behavior, but today *chastity* has pretty much reverted to simply meaning "abstinence from sexual activity."

Cheesecake

*C*heesecake is one of those words that would be a lot easier to explain if we had a working time machine. Way back in the 1930s, long before the Internet and cable TV put "hard core" on the national menu, tabloid newspapers and disreputable "pulp" magazines would often try to attract their largely male target audience by festooning their front page with photographs of attractive young women displaying especially attractive parts of their anatomy. This being the 1930s, such displays were tame by modern standards and usually limited to what were known as *leg shots,* featuring young women in swimsuits or relatively short skirts. Similar tableaux were common on calendars and playing cards of the period, and the genre was known among aficionados as *cheesecake.* (Among non-aficionados it was usually condemned as *smut.*)

Cheesecake in the literal sense is, of course, a rich dessert made of cream cheese, eggs, butter, and sugar. When their mouths are not full of the stuff, devotees of cheesecake spend

Skin-Deep

I'm tired of all this nonsense about beauty being
only skin-deep. That's deep enough. What do you
want—an adorable pancreas? —Jean Kerr

There's a lot to be said for valuing superficial beauty. After all, while you may know that your beloved is kind, considerate, loving, and faithful, none of that is going to turn heads on the beach, and none of your friends is really likely to envy you and your date's *intellectual compatibility.*

Besides, there's no need to feel superficial when you've got history on your side. Take a good look at all those old statues and vases and even prehistoric cave paintings and what do you see? Knockouts and lookers, from the sculptures of ancient Greece to the cover of last week's *People* magazine. It's all biology, of course—call it *survival of the cutest.* Naturally, the English language has been doing its best through the ages to fine-tune the vocabulary of pulchritude.

Pretty: When we inherited *pretty* from Old English, it meant "cunning," "crafty," or "deceitful," reflecting its origins in the Old English *praett,* or "trick." By the fifteenth century, however, we were using *pretty* to mean "well-made" or "clever," from which it developed senses of "fine," "agreeable," or "excellent." During this period, *pretty* was often applied to men, in the sense of "brave" or "gallant." Eventually, *pretty* took on its modern meaning of "possessing beauty," but it carries overtones of daintiness compared to the more substantial *beautiful.*

Beautiful: The root of *beauty,* which entered English in the thirteenth century, is the Latin word for "beautiful," *bellus,* the change in spelling coming from its having filtered through French for a few centuries. *Beautiful,* which showed up in the sixteenth century, has always meant "full of beauty" and has been used to describe everything from a very attractive woman (rarely are men called *beautiful*) to a mathematical theorem. Occasionally, *beautiful* takes on an iconic, abstract, and even cynical tone, as in the term *beautiful people,* used to describe celebrities whose actual beauty in any notable sense is debatable.

Handsome: The original meaning of *handsome,* when it appeared in English around 1435, was not "masculine," "rugged," "suave," "stylish," or any of its other modern synonyms. *Handsome* meant "easy to manipulate or use," reflecting its origin as a combination of *hand* with the suffix *some,* meaning "amenable to" (much as *toothsome* means "delicious"). A good saw was called *handsome.* For the next few centuries, *handsome* acquired the broader meanings of "graceful," "generous," "courteous," "admirable," and so forth, until it took on its current meaning of "having a fine, stately figure or appearance" in the late sixteenth century. Until the mid–twentieth century, *handsome* was applied to women as well as men, but a man describing his wife as *handsome* today would probably be making a serious mistake.

Gorgeous: It may not be wise to judge a book by its cover, but *gorgeous* reflects that impulse as applied to people. Borrowed from the Old French *gorgias* (meaning "elegantly dressed") in the late fifteenth century, *gorgeous* originally meant "adorned in brilliant colors," "showy," or "magnificent," and when applied to a woman, it referred specifically to her clothes, not her personal beauty. Today, of course, *gorgeous* is frequently applied to women wearing few, if any, clothes.

Skin Deep continued

Lovely: If you take *lovely* apart, its original meaning emerges. The suffix *ly* means, in this case, "characteristic of" or "befitting"; thus *lovely,* which appeared around A.D. 1000, originally meant "loving," "kind," and "affectionate." It also meant "lovable," "worthy of love," and, more important, "attractive to love," which by the fourteenth century had blossomed into the modern meaning of *lovely:* "attractive because of great beauty; very beautiful." Women and girls are most often described as *lovely,* although men are sometimes termed *lovely* by women who do not know them well.

Fetching: It's a tribute to the flexibility of the English language that a term for the action of a dog chasing a Frisbee could also be an adjective describing an attractive young woman. The basic meaning of *fetch,* which is rooted in the Old English *fetian,* is "go and get," and for most of its history, *fetch* meant simply various forms of going and getting. Starting in the early seventeenth century, however, *fetch* acquired the extended meaning of "to interest or attract." The adjective *fetching* appeared in the nineteenth century, meaning "alluring," "fascinating," or "irresistibly attractive," and today it is used to describe a woman whose appearance reaches out and grabs men.

Cute: When *cute* first appeared in the early eighteenth century, the observation "He's cute but not very bright" would have made no sense at all. *Cute* is actually a cropped (or *aphetic*) form of the adjective *acute,* and the original sense of *cute* was "clever," "sharp," or "shrewd." This sense is still heard in that staple of crime-movie dialogue, "Don't try anything cute." By the early twentieth century, cute was taking on its modern meaning of "attractive" or "charming," often notably lacking the old connotation of "sharp."

most of their time debating the source of the best cheesecake, with Junior's Restaurant in Brooklyn being a perennial nominee. But how did *cheesecake* come to be a synonym for female pulchritude employed as an advertising gambit?

The answer probably lies in the fact that, although real cheesecake was invented back in the fifteenth century, *cheesecake* as a slang term first arose in the depths of the 1930s depression. Having enough food to eat was a daily worry for millions of Americans, so cheesecake, or any other fancy dessert, would have seemed an unattainable luxury to many. It's not surprising that the young women on the covers of those risqué magazines, similarly unattainable to the average reader, would have become known as *cheesecake.*

Of course, what's good for the gander often works for the goose as well, so by the 1940s Hollywood had discovered that *beefcake*—images of muscular, often shirtless, male actors—greatly boosted box-office interest among women. Playfully coined on the model of *cheesecake, beefcake* substitutes *beef,* popular slang for "muscular power" or "strength" (as in "a beefy man") since the mid–nineteenth century. There is, of course, no actual food called *beefcake,* the closest thing probably being the notably unsexy meatloaf. But it is unlikely that any woman has ever confused beefcake with meatloaf.

How did
CHEESECAKE come
to be a synonym for
female pulchritude
employed as an
advertising gambit?

Chivalry

The remarkable thing about chivalry is that it has regularly been pronounced dead almost since the day it was born, but like the Energizer Bunny, it just keeps on going. The current state of chivalry is, as usual, a subject of some dispute. Chivalry, however, once meant far more than a man opening a door for a woman.

Back in the feudal world of the eleventh century, the popular heroes were not athletes or even actors, but the valiant knights of the Crusades. Epic poems and songs in France extolled the bravery and virtue of the *chevalier* or *cavalier* (from the Latin *caballarus,* "horseman" or "knight," also the source of *cavalry*), and *chevalerie,* the high moral code by which knights lived, was widely admired. This code demanded not only bravery in battle, but honesty and courtesy in all aspects of daily life, especially toward women.

By the time *chevaleros* (meaning possessing "knightly qualities") appeared in English as *chevalrous* in the fourteenth century, actual knights had become quite rare, and the word fell into disuse. But nostalgia for the good old days of knighthood and valor during the seventeenth and eighteenth centuries revitalized *chivalry,* at least as a concept.

The remarkable thing about chivalry is that it has regularly been pronounced dead almost since the day it was born, but like the Energizer Bunny, it just keeps on going.

The rise of modern warfare in the early twentieth century, with its capacity for mass, impersonal slaughter, put an end to any lingering traces of chivalry on the battlefield, but the concept of honor and restraint in civilian life held on, arguably, until the latter part of the century. Today *chivalry,* once the demanding moral code of knights, has become synonymous with simple "politeness."

Concupiscence

First things first. A racy word is no fun at all if we can't pronounce it, and *concupiscence* is a real tongue twister. The trick is to keep the syllables separate: "kon-KYOO-pih-sense." A little practice a few times a day will ensure proper pronunciation within a week at most.

Then again, why bother? *Concupiscence* is really just a ten-dollar synonym for good old-fashioned "lust," drawn directly from the Latin *concupiscere,* meaning "to desire vehemently or ardently." For whatever reason—its length, its unpronounceability, or its sheer Latinate fussiness—*concupiscence* is rarely seen or heard outside of historical novels and Sunday morning talking-head shows. So unless your ambition is to hear your friends exclaim, "Gee, you sound just like George Will!" you can probably skip *concupiscence* and stick to *the hots.*

CONCUPISCENCE is really just a ten-dollar synonym for good old-fashioned "lust."

Conjugal

Married couples who sometimes feel that they are yoked together can take some comfort in the fact that such relentless togetherness goes a long way back. *Conjugal,* meaning "pertaining to marriage; concerning the relationship of husband and wife," is rooted in the Latin *conjugare,* which means "to join together in matrimony." So far, so good. But trace *conjugare* back a bit, and we discover that it arose as a combination of *com,* "together," and *jugare,* meaning "to yoke," as a farmer might yoke together a team of oxen. The root of *jugare,* the Indo-European *jugom,* also gave modern English the words *yoke* and *yoga* (from the Sanskrit *yoga,* meaning "union with the universal spirit"), as well as *join* and *junction. Conjugal* first appeared in English around 1545 and is used today primarily in legal contexts, as in the term *conjugal visits.* In more informal contexts, the same "yoked together" principle is conveyed by the slang term *ball and chain.*

CONJUGAL arose as a combination of COM, "together," and JUGARE, meaning "to yoke," as a farmer might yoke together a team of oxen.

Coo

When a bird (especially a dove or a pigeon) coos, it is making the soft, musical murmuring sound characteristic of its species. No one knows why birds coo. For all we know, they could be discussing sports scores. But the cooing of birds has become a powerful metaphor in our language of love. For humans, *to coo* in the romantic sense means "to converse amorously, usually in softly murmuring tones, with one's beloved." In both senses, the word *coo* is what linguists call *echoic* or *imitative* in origin, meaning that *coo* arose (around 1670) as an attempt to imitate the sound made by doves or pigeons.

Coo in the human sweet-nothings sense is also found in the phrase *bill and coo,* modeled again on the behavior of doves, who often caress each other with their bills while cooing. (By *bills,* of course, we mean the birds' beaks. Bills in the context of human relationships rarely inspire cooing.)

Coquette

The *Oxford English Dictionary* defines *coquette* as "a woman (more or less young), who uses arts to gain the admiration and affection of men, merely for the gratification of vanity or from a desire of conquest, and without any intention of responding to the feelings aroused; a woman who habitually trifles with the affections of men; a flirt."

To achieve her nefarious goals, the coquette employs the arts of flirtation, techniques and tactics that may, depending on the target, range from avowing a love of Bartók to feigning an interest in the Cleveland Browns football team. Given, however, the short attention span of the average coquette, the target will almost inevitably be left, after a few weeks (or in extreme cases, mere hours), with an extra season ticket to something he will likely never be able to enjoy again.

Coquette is French, drawn from *coq,* meaning "rooster." There was, as you may suspect, a missing link, an intermediate epithet, betwixt "male chicken" and "female flirt." It was the now-obsolete male form *coquet,* a linguistic tribute to the strutting, henhouse-Lothario antics of the rooster. Although both *coquet* and *coquette* appeared in English in the seventeenth century, only *coquette* has survived in our language, possibly because the male *coquet* is now known as a *jerk.*

Courtship

C*ourtship,* the process of wooing one's beloved toward the goal of marriage, is like a trip to Disney World: days of eager expectation heightening to near apoplexy for all parties involved, followed by standing, at least metaphorically, in a very long line for a very long time.

And in the end, if you're lucky, you get to pose for a picture with Goofy.

OK, scratch that whole simile. But if it's any comfort to those going through the process, courtship, which today usually amounts to some initially awkward restaurant meals and maybe a few movies, used to be much more stressful. When *courtship* first appeared in English (apparently invented by Shakespeare in his play *Love's Labors Lost,* circa 1588), it meant "behavior befitting a member of a royal court," with all the stiffness, florid language, and demonstrations of subservience that hanging out with a monarch required. Such courtly behavior was also expected of a proper gentleman's approach to a lady whose hand he desired in marriage, and by the end of the sixteenth century this highly formal process of wooing came to be called *courtship* or simply *courting.*

Crush

Crush is a deceptive little word. We all know the giddy feeling of a sudden infatuation, the dreamy fantasies, the golden pedestal on which we place our new beloved (crushes are nearly always a phenomenon of "the new"). And *crush* even sounds like the rush of love at first sight and the tidal wave of infatuation that marks the state of having a crush on someone. But while *crush* may sound frivolous and even silly, an argument could be made that without crushes our economy would collapse. Think of the florists, the

An argument could be made that without crushes our economy would collapse.

greeting-card companies, and the jewelers, the restaurants, movie theaters, Broadway shows, haberdashers, and hairdressers, not to mention credit card companies and therapists, whose existence would be threatened by the abolition (if such a thing were possible) of the crush. The drop in aftershave and cologne sales alone would put a significant dent in the GNP.

No one knows exactly where the use of *crush* to denote "a romantic infatuation" came from. In the early nineteenth century, *crush* was used as a colloquial term for a very crowded social gathering, such as a dance or a party, probably because the claustrophobia quotient was fairly high at such affairs. It is possible that when *crush* in the love sense first appeared, around 1884, it was somehow connected to this sort of social occasion. In any case, crushes are usually temporary phenomena, which is a good thing: if allowed to go on too long, the average crush would end in crushing bankruptcy.

Cuckold

Go ahead: blame it on the birds. One of the more shameful themes in human language has been our eagerness to liken our most unfortunate characteristics to the behavior of animals who, in most cases,

wouldn't be caught dead acting like humans. For centuries, *drunk as a skunk* has slandered the sober skunk, *dog in the manger* has maligned the noble and generous dog, and *loony* has defamed the eminently sane loon. By this point the entire animal kingdom must be silently shouting, "Oh yeah? Well, you're a bigger one!"

Cuckold is, as the *Oxford English Dictionary* delicately puts it, "a derisive name for the husband of an unfaithful wife" and can also be used as a verb meaning "to dishonor a husband by committing adultery." Although the shame and scandal attached to *cuckold* are purely human conceits, we named it, true to form, by scrounging around for an animal metaphor, in this case the innocent cuckoo. A *cuckoo* is a small European bird known (and named) for its

One of the more shameful themes in human language has been our eagerness to liken our most unfortunate characteristics to the behavior of animals.

charming *coo-coo-coo* call. The cuckoo is also notable for the female cuckoo's habit of laying her eggs in other birds' nests. It was this practice that apparently reminded the French back in the fifteenth century of the behavior of certain human females. Although men are statistically more likely to be unfaithful, *cuckold* remains a gender-specific term with no real equivalent for an aggrieved female. While the verb *to cuckold* refers to the behavior of the faithless woman, *cuckold* as a noun is reserved for the deceived—or "cuckolded"—man.

Cuddle

Cuddle means "to hug or embrace closely and affectionately," "to nestle with another person," or "to curl up warm and snug to go to sleep." *Cuddle* has been common in English since the sixteenth century, and it's possible that *cuddle* is based on the word *couth,* which originally meant "well-known" or "familiar" and only gradually acquired the current meaning of "agreeable and pleasant." *Couth* is, of course, most commonly employed in its antonym, *uncouth,* meaning "rude," "rough," or "uncivilized," all of which would certainly make a person uncuddlable.

Cupid

When the Romans took many of the ancient Greek gods as their own, Aphrodite, the Greek goddess of love, had her name changed to Venus, and her son Eros ended up with the somewhat dorky moniker *Cupid.* Unlike the other gods, who were generally represented as adults, Cupid was given the form of a winged infant armed with a bow and arrows. Cupid's shtick was to fly around and shoot his invisible love arrows into the hearts of mortals, thus causing the poor saps to fall passionately in love. *To be struck by Cupid's arrow* is an antiquated metaphor for the onset of such a sudden infatuation.

Cupid most often appears these days

The name KEWPIE was a modification of CUPID.

as a fixture on Valentine's Day cards, but students of the tackier precincts of popular culture will remember Kewpie dolls, which, during one period in early twentieth century America, were as wildly popular as teddy bears. The invention of a commercial illustrator named Rose O'Neill, the Kewpie doll consisted of a standard-issue beatific baby doll with the addition of wings and a topknot. Long after the public rage for Kewpie dolls had abated, O'Neill's invention remained the nearly inevitable prize in carnival games. The name *Kewpie* was, as you may by now suspect, a modification of *Cupid*.

Dalliance

Do not, as some ungracious pastors do,
Show me the steep and thorny way to heaven,
Whiles, like a puff'd and reckless libertine,
Himself the primrose path of dalliance treads,
And reaks [heeds] not his own rede [advice].

—William Shakespeare, *Hamlet*

You go, girl. What Ophelia was trying to say to her brother, Laertes, was that girls just wanna have fun. A little romantic dalliance never hurt anyone.

A *dalliance* is a light, frivolous amorous encounter, perhaps a little more serious than a flirtation, but certainly not an affair. At the root of *dalliance* lies the verb *to dally*, from the Old French *dalier*, meaning

A little romantic dalliance never hurt anyone.

"to chat, converse, pass the time." Today we usually use *dally* (often in the form *dillydally*) in a negative sense to mean "to linger, loiter, or waste time," but when *dally* first appeared around 1300 it meant simply "to chat or spend time with friends." *Dalliance* today means time spent with one very special friend.

Darling

D*arling* is probably the most popular endearment in the English language, and one of the oldest, to boot, having first appeared around A.D. 888 in the early form *deorling*. *Darling* is a versatile word, too, commonly used as a noun meaning "a person who is loved," an adjective meaning "loved," and an affectionate form of address ("Darling, fetch me another bonbon, please"). *Darling* can also be used in a figurative (and often slightly sarcastic) sense to mean one who is favored or preferred by a person or entity not usually considered affectionate ("The president is the darling of the oil companies").

> DARLING is probably the most popular endearment in the
> English language, and one of the oldest, to boot, having
> first appeared around A.D. 888 in the early form DEORLING.

Date

First things first: the *date* you accompany to the movies has nothing to do with the *date* that grows on trees. The fruit kind of *date* takes its name from the Greek *dactylus,* meaning "finger" or "toe," as the Greeks evidently detected a resemblance between the chewy dates and their toes. Go figure.

Date in the sense of "the precise time something takes place" comes from the way Romans dated their letters. It was customary to begin with the phrase *Data Romae,* "Given at Rome," followed by the day and month. Eventually *data* came to be used as shorthand for the time notation itself, passed into French as *date,* and was adopted into English in the same *date* form in the fourteenth century. *Date* had acquired the derivative sense of "an appointment or engagement at a particular time, especially with a member of the opposite sex" by the nineteenth century, and *to date* in this sense had become a verb by 1902, but the practice of referring to the person one was meeting as *a date* is more recent, having first appeared around 1925.

Dear John Letter

There are worse things out there in the postal system than junk mail, and one of them has been a fixture of life since the Second World War: the Dear John letter. A *Dear John letter* is a missive penned by one's paramour in which she (or he) abruptly announces an end to the relationship. *Dear John letter* entered the public vocabulary via the military during World War II, a conflict that sent millions of husbands and boyfriends overseas, many of whom discovered that absence, especially prolonged for years, often does *not* make the heart grow fonder. As a Rochester, New York, newspaper explained in 1947:

"'Dear John,' the letter began. 'I have found someone else whom I think the world of. I think the only way out is for us to get a divorce,' it said. They usually began like that, those letters that told of infidelity on the part of the wives of servicemen. . . . The men called them 'Dear Johns.'"

The pain of receiving such a letter in the midst of a war in a faraway land must have been made all the worse by the stilted salutation apparently common in such messages—"Dear John," rather than the expected "Dear Johnny," "My Dearest John," or simply "Darling"—and probably explains how the *Dear John letter* came to stand for the entire phenomenon of long-distance postal dumping.

A *Dear John letter* may also be the key to another popular phrase, *that's all she wrote,* meaning "that's all there is" or "that's the end of it." According to some authorities, a joke current among servicemen during World War II had a soldier opening a letter and reading it aloud to his com-

There are worse things out there in the postal system than junk mail, and one of them has been a fixture of life since the Second World War: the Dear John letter.

rades. "Dear John," he reads, and then abruptly stops. His mates urge him to go on reading. "That's all she wrote," he says, holding up the letter, which is blank except for the deadly salutation.

Divorce

Not every love story has a happy ending, as evidenced by the fact that marriage in the twenty-first-century United States has at least a fifty-fifty chance of eventually ending in divorce, the legal, permanent dissolution of marriage bonds. But while divorce may be initiated by either party to the marriage, women apparently had the idea first. English adopted *divorce* way back in 1377 (in the form *devors*) from the Old French *divorce,* which in turn was based on the Latin *divertium,* "separation," or "dissolution of marriage," drawn from the Latin verb *divertere,* which was applied mainly to women and meant "to turn away" or "to leave one's husband." Then again, the same verb gave us the modern English verb *to divert,* and many divorces have been caused by husbands being *diverted* from their wives by other women.

While divorce may be initiated by either party to the marriage, women apparently had the idea first.

Dote

If you happen to be among the lucky married folk who are blessed with a doting mate who caters to your every whim, a word of warning: you might want to keep him or her away from sharp objects.

Dote is one of those English words, like *infatuation,* that reveal our ambiguous view of romantic attachment: in moderation, love is grand, but a smidgen too much caring and you're considered a candidate for the funny farm.

Today we usually hear *dote* in the sense of "to be infatuatedly fond of; to lavish affection and attention upon" (as in "Larry doted on Diana and was never happier than when peeling her a grape").

But when English borrowed *doten* from Middle Dutch in the thirteenth century, the connotation was a bit less romantic: *dote* originally meant "silly," "foolish," "stupid," or "deranged." A *dotard* (one who dotes) was a foolish or silly person, especially one whose mental faculties had been impaired by advancing age. This sense of *dote* persists today largely in derivatives such as *dotage,* meaning "senility" (as in "The fact that Larry had entered his dotage became evident when he began stuffing peeled grapes in his ears"), and *dotty,* meaning "deranged by age."

The modern sense of *dote,* meaning "to love and care for attentively," appeared in the late fifteenth century, an outgrowth of the original "foolish" connotation. *To dote* today is to be silly and maybe even a little crazy, but all in the noble cause of love.

Ecstasy

Ecstasy comes from *ekstasis,* a Greek word meaning "out of one's mind," and means "a state of passionate delirium." *Ecstasy,* imported into English via Old French in the fourteenth century, was an early form of the insanity defense. People in the grip of romantic ecstasy have traditionally been forgiven all sorts of lapses, from forgetting to feed the goldfish to forgetting that they are married to someone other than the object of their ecstasy.

> ECSTASY, imported to English via Old French in the fourteenth century, was an early form of the insanity defense.

Elope

Let's just elope" is a thought that probably occurs at some point to every couple facing the tidal wave of anxiety and hoopla that accompanies a large family wedding. And dozens of Hollywood comedies have included a scene of the daring swain appearing with a ladder under his beloved's bedroom window late at night. But eloping, today the symbol of free-spirited lovers flouting society's stodgy expectations, was once not such a laughing matter. It was, in fact, a crime.

In the seventeenth century, *elopement* was a legal term applied to a married woman who ran away from her husband with her lover. *Elope* was formed from the Middle English *alopen,* past participle of *aleapen,* formed from *a,* "away," plus *leap,* the same as our modern word *leap.* So a woman who eloped was figuratively (and, depending on the timing of her departure, possibly literally) leaping away from her legal husband and was in a peck of trouble if and when he caught up with her.

While a married woman still occasionally runs away with her lover to escape her marriage, the term *elope* has undergone a sense change and even a slight reversal since the nineteenth century, and is now usually applied to two unmarried lovers who run away in order to get married. Parental objections to the union are a common motive for eloping, but some couples probably head for the hills just to avoid addressing all those wedding invitations.

Enthrall

Although today we use *enthrall* to mean "to captivate or hold spellbound by means of agreeable qualities" ("Larry was enthralled by every aspect of Cindy, especially her last name, which happened to be Budweiser"), the original sense was considerably less cheerful. The root of *enthrall,* which first appeared in English in the sixteenth century, is *thrall,* an archaic term with Germanic roots, meaning "captive" or "slave." In feudal times, for instance, a serf was said to be *in thrall,* "in legal and economic bondage," to his lord or master.

By Shakespeare's time, however, *enthrall* was most often used in the modern figurative sense to mean "to captivate or fascinate," often in a romantic or sexual sense, as in "So is mine eye enthralled to thy shape," from *A Midsummer Night's Dream.*

The root of ENTHRALL is THRALL, an archaic term with Germanic roots meaning "captive" or "slave."

Erotic

It's a bird! It's a plane! No, it's another annoying flying matchmaker.

In Greek mythology, Eros was the son of Aphrodite, the goddess of love. Lacking any real job, Eros was a spoiled youth who spent his time flying around mischievously shooting love arrows at mortals, causing the poor fools to be seized with uncontrollable sexual passion. (If this sounds familiar, it's because when the Romans appropriated the Greek gods as their own, Aphrodite became Venus, and Eros was transformed into the ubiquitous cute winged baby we know as Cupid.)

A cynic would say that erotica is just porn created for people with graduate degrees.

As a symbol of carnal passion, Eros was a hit, and *erotic* has been used in English to mean "pertaining to or inspiring sexual passion or lust" since the seventeenth century. The related word *erotica,* meaning "sexually stimulating writing or illustrations," is often differentiated from *pornography,* but a cynic would say that erotica is just porn created for people with graduate degrees.

Facts of Life

The Greeks had a word for it: *euphemismos,* meaning "the use of a pleasant word in place of an unpleasantly blunt, but perhaps more accurate, term." Our everyday English is full of euphemisms that let us sidestep the big no-no's of polite conversation: death, religion, money, and a wide variety of bodily functions, most especially sex. We speak of *making love* when we usually mean "copulating" and of our *significant other* on those occasions when the simple "lover" would seem too blunt.

All euphemisms are simply fig leaves—even most children know that when Fluffy is *put to sleep* she isn't likely to wake up soon. But *facts of life,* common since the late nineteenth century, is a phrase so vague it might well refer to the force of gravity or income tax, and it does a bang-up job of confusing many children. So, on the off chance that a few readers' parents never quite got around to explaining the facts of life to them, here's the sordid truth: *the facts of life* means "S-E-X."

Faithful

Faith is ultimately about *trust*. The root of *faith* is the Latin *fides*, which also gave us, among other English words, *fidelity, confide,* and the perfect name for a faithful dog, *Fido*. The basic sense of *faith* when it first appeared in English in the thirteenth century was "trust" or "belief." Religious faith, the faith one shows toward one's neighbors and associates, the faith one keeps in carrying out the promises of love and marriage, all involve trust and belief, ideally absolute and unwavering.

All of which brings us to the private eye staking out a motel by the airport where his client's wayward spouse is about to be proved unfaithful. The original sense of *faithful* when it appeared in English around 1300 was simply "full of faith," usually of the religious variety. A more general sense soon developed, in which the faithful person was not just trusting but trustworthy—true to his or her beliefs and bound by the promises he or she made. By 1400, the word *unfaithful,* which had been coined as a religious synonym for *infidel,* was being used to describe a person who broke secular promises and betrayed confidences. As the most solemn promises that most people made were their marriage vows of fidelity, *unfaithful* came to be applied to a person who betrayed his or her spouse by engaging in sexual activity outside the marriage. Oddly enough, although adultery is certainly not a recent invention, the term *unfaithful* was not applied to the offending spouse until the early nineteenth century, possibly because until that point it was still primarily used in its religious sense.

Nudge, Nudge, Wink, Wink

Human beings spend a lot of time and effort *not* saying what they mean. The urge to substitute a tamer term for one that might offend is far from new; the term for such linguistic diplomacy was coined by the ancient Greeks: *euphemism,* from *eu,* meaning "sounding good," and *pheme,* "speech."

Euphemisms function as verbal code words in the great game of social propriety, allowing polite people to discuss touchy subjects while maintaining a respectable distance—what the CIA would call deniability—from the taboo subject. Euphemisms are almost always either overtly deceptive (*collateral damage,* meaning "dead civilians") or coyly ambiguous (*rest room*).

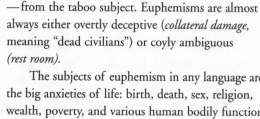

The subjects of euphemism in any language are the big anxieties of life: birth, death, sex, religion, wealth, poverty, and various human bodily functions. The heyday of euphemisms in English, especially those concerned with matters sexual, was the nineteenth-century reign of Queen Victoria in Britain, when linguistic prudery reached such a high pitch that the *breast* of a chicken became *white meat,* the *leg* of a fowl became the *drumstick* (the *legs* of humans became *limbs*), and *bulls* became *gentleman cows.* But Victorian England was merely building on a rage for euphemisms that had started in the seventeenth century and continues to this day.

Future connoisseurs of irony will note that the twenty-first century began with both unprecedented frankness about sexual behavior in the mass media *and* a large repertoire of euphemisms, some old, some new, many borrowed, but none blue, regarding even the most prosaic manifestations of sexuality. Here is a sampling of our modern weasel words.

Adult: When used in terms such as *adult communities, adult* is a euphemism for "old." But append *adult* to *books, films,* or *TV programming,* and it's a code word for "sexual" or "sexually explicit." The opposite of *adult* in the sexual sense is *family* (as in the term *family programming*), although families would be fairly scarce were it not for adult behavior.

Affair: In a general sense, *affair* is one of the broadest nouns in English, meaning simply "a thing," "a matter between people," or "something done," reflecting its roots in the Old French phrase *à faire,* meaning "to do." In the context of romance, however, an *affair* is a sexual relationship, usually illicit in some respect, of a duration somewhere between a one-night stand and, well, a long-term affair.

All the Way: Sexual intercourse, the home run of the classic teenage baseball hierarchy of sexual activity: first base (necking), second base (fondling, perhaps more), and third base (anything short of intercourse). *All the way* has faded from the teen vocabulary in recent years and is heard today mostly from the lips of aging umpires.

Altogether, in the: Naked. Also called *au naturel* (French for "in the natural state," originally a cooking term for food served without a sauce), *in one's birthday suit,* and *in the buff* (from the similarity in color of human skin to buffalo hide).

Bastard: A child born outside of wedlock. From the Old French *fils de bast,* or "packsaddle child," meaning that conception took place in informal circumstances, possibly during an encounter with a passing cowherd. *Bastard* is an anomaly—a euphemism that, ironically, became a swearword. When *bastard* first appeared in the thirteenth century, it was considered less harsh than the alternative *whoreson,* and the word wasn't employed as an insult until the eighteenth century. William the Conqueror (William I, king of England), for instance, was commonly known as ☞

Nudge, Nudge, Wink, Wink continued

William the Bastard. *Bastard* was considered a heavy-duty swearword (roughly equivalent to *son of a bitch,* another illegitimacy reference) for most of the twentieth century and is only now emerging into acceptable use on television.

Conjugal: From the Latin *con,* "together," and *jugere,* "to join." Strictly speaking, *conjugal* is a catchall term meaning "pertaining to husband and wife and relations between them." But in common usage since prisoners in penitentiaries in the United States raised the demand for "conjugal visits" in the 1970s, *conjugal* has been an official euphemism for sexual activity between married couples.

Exotic Dancer: A stripper, a euphemism courtesy of the self-respect movement among "sex workers" that began in the 1970s. Whether *exotic dancer* is classier than the previous euphemism *ecdysiast* (coined by H. L. Mencken in 1940 from the scientific term for the act of molting an outer layer, such as skin) is debatable, but it is far easier to pronounce.

Extramarital: Adulterous, meaning literally "outside the marriage." An early-twentieth-century replacement of a morally judgmental term with a geographical one.

Intimate: Referring to sexual behavior, usually employed when such relations are illicit. From the Latin adjective *intimus,* meaning "most profound" or "close" (as in "an intimate friend"), *intimate* was first applied in the seventeenth century to very close friends or similar relationships. *Intimate* became a euphemism for sexual intercourse in the late nineteenth century in the usage *intimate with.* While euphemisms probably cannot be said to possess self-consciousness, it is intriguing that *intimate* is also a verb meaning "to hint at."

Make Love: To engage in sexual intercourse. Until the late nineteenth century, *to make love* was quite a bit tamer, usually referring to courting or pitching woo and sometimes to what we would just consider flirting today. The original sense, dating back to the sixteenth century, was literally "to make someone love you; to inspire love in another."

Relationship: Another term so general (meaning "the state of being related in some respect") that only context (and added modifiers such as *personal* or *close*) can signal the difference between a relationship with one's spouse and a relationship with one's cable TV company (which may be why so many husbands seem to confuse the two). As a euphemism, a *relationship* is almost always a long-term affair, sometimes involving cohabitation by the couple (also known as *live-in lovers*).

Sex Worker: Most often a prostitute, though the category can include strippers, porn stars, and some massage parlor personnel. *Sex worker,* which dates back to the 1970s, might best be termed an *in-your-face euphemism,* the function of which is not to hide the nature of the job but to defend it and demand that it be granted the same respect as other occupations.

Sleep With: To engage in sexual intercourse with. Best of breed in the world of euphemisms, *to sleep with* is a stunning achievement in that it says nearly the opposite of what it means (frequently very little sleeping is done on such occasions), yet everyone understands exactly what is really meant. A coinage the modern public relations industry can only envy, *sleep with* has been in common use since at least the early nineteenth century, but *sleep* in various combinations has been used as a euphemism for "have sex" since A.D. 900.

Fawn

The lover who fawns over his beloved, showering her with gifts, plying her with flowers and candy, and catering to her every whim and fancy, need not take time from his amorous duties to wonder what his behavior has to do with a baby deer. Notwithstanding the love Bambi's mother bore for her fawn, there is no connection between the verb *to fawn,* meaning "to care for fondly; to delight in the presence of," and the deer sort of *fawn,* which came in a roundabout way from the Latin *fetus,* meaning "offspring."

The human verb *to fawn* is actually a variant of the much older English verb *fain,* which meant "to be glad" or "to rejoice" and survives only in the antiquated adverb form *fain,* meaning "willingly," which today appears largely in historical dramas (as in "I would fain marry thee, were thou not a vile varlet").

When *fawn* first appeared in English around 1225, it was as an intransitive verb meaning "to show delight or fondness," and was specifically applied to dogs fawning by wagging their tails. Within a century or so, *fawn* was being applied to people, meaning "to caress and attentively care for another person." But *fawn* still carried a hint of canine servility, in the sense that *to fawn* was to demean oneself (like a dog) in order to curry favor. Today the connotation of *fawn* depends on the fawnee: to fawn on one's boss is craven and demeaning, but to fawn on one's mate is considered romantic (and in fact, failing to fawn may land you in the doghouse).

Fickle

One minute they love you; the next, they don't. One day they want to meet your parents; the next, they ignore you on the elevator. Welcome to the world of the fickle, where relationships bite the dust for no good reason at all.

When *fickle* (from the Old English *ficol*) first appeared in English in the thirteenth century, it meant "deceitful" or "treacherous." Fairly quickly, however, *fickle* took on the narrower sense of "changeable, inconstant, and unreliable." Pretty soon, folks began to notice that much of life, including such basics things as fortune, popularity, and health (not to mention lottery numbers) were fickle. Shakespeare even complained of life's fickleness in *Romeo and Juliet:* "O Fortune, Fortune, all men call thee fickle."

But while most of us have come to accept the Fickle Finger of Fate and its illogical choices, the fickle lover who changes his or her mind on a whim remains perhaps the most painful pitfall of love. After all, Fate may screw you out of winning the lottery, but you don't forever after have to walk past Fate's desk to get to the watercooler.

Flattery

There is flattery in friendship," noted Shakespeare in *Henry V,* and that goes double for love and romance. Being asked for a date is flattering, as is acceptance for the asker; being asked or accepted for another date is still more; and every subsequent yes in the burgeoning relationship is a boost to the self-esteem of both parties. Romance is in large part a festival of mutual admiration, and the whole little circus runs on a constant give-and-take of flattery. Many people probably get married just to be able to relax.

Since flattery consists in large part of ego-stroking, it's appropriate that the word's origin lies in real stroking. The root of *flatter,* which entered English in the thirteenth century, was the Old French *flater,* which meant "to caress or flatten with one's hand" (and is closely related to the word *flat*). Along with the literal "stroke" sense of *flatter* we also imported a figurative sense of the French word, "to praise or compliment excessively or insincerely," as if the flatterer were petting or stroking the flatteree like a pampered pet.

The connotations of *flattery* (the act or product of flattering) have varied over the word's history in English. Some senses stress the insincerity of flattery, while other, later uses seem to regard flattery as simply a nice way to inspire or encourage friendship or love. But the bottom line is that flattery works because, as Dame Edith Sitwell once observed, "The aim of flattery is to soothe and encourage us by assuring us of the truth of an opinion we have already formed about ourselves."

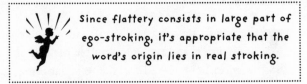

Since flattery consists in large part of ego-stroking, it's appropriate that the word's origin lies in real stroking.

Flirt

To *flirt* in modern usage is "to make playful romantic or sexual overtures to another person." The key word in this definition is *playful*—flirting done properly always leaves the door open for one to simply walk away without further ado, let alone marriage.

Oddly enough, when *flirt* first appeared in English around 1553, it meant "to sneer or scoff at; to turn up one's nose at; to snub"—hardly the sort of behavior that would lead to a date. At about the same time, *flirt* was also used to mean "a flick of the finger" or "a light tap or slap," possibly reflecting the origins of *flirt,* like those of *flick* and *slap,* as an imitation of a natural sound.

By the late sixteenth century, *to flirt* meant "to move in a jerky fashion" or "to constantly flit from one subject to another," as a butterfly might dart from flower to flower. Thus, by the eighteenth century, *to flirt* had arrived at its modern meaning, and *flirt* as a noun had come to mean "a person who makes a habit of getting other people worked up with no intention of forming a lasting relationship."

Fornication

The scene: the reception after the wedding of the family's eldest daughter. The bride's mother is approached by her youngest, a girl of six. "Momma," the little girl asks, "what does *fornication* mean?" Surprised, her mother asks where she heard the word. "From Grandma," the girl replies. "Your grandmother said that? Are you sure?" asks the shocked mother. "Yes, she did," says the child. "Grandma said, 'Fornication like this, we should have hired a better band.'"

For a word that describes one of the major taboos of human society, *fornication* has been sufficiently tamed by liberalized social norms in recent decades that jokes like the above can be told with little fear of giving offense. But the inventors of the word *fornication* were seriously determined to stamp out the practice. The Latin word *fornix* meant "arch" or "vault," and in the late Roman period the term was used to mean the cavernous underground passages beneath Rome where vagrants, criminals, and prostitutes tended to congregate. Early Christian writers, condemning the prostitution taking place there, used *fornix* to mean "brothel," which spawned the verb *fornicare,* meaning "to have illicit sexual intercourse." In English, *fornication* appeared in the thirteenth century, originally meaning "voluntary sexual intercourse between an unmarried man and an unmarried woman." Strictly speaking, adultery, involving at least one partner who was married to someone else, was therefore not fornication (not that the distinction made much difference in eras when both were illegal). In modern use, however, *fornication* generally refers to any combination of married or unmarried participants. But not surprisingly, as the activity itself has become less scandalous, the word has faded from the public vocabulary. Today the term *fornication* is most likely to be invoked in the fire-and-brimstone pronouncements of religious conservatives, who remain opposed to it, no matter how good the band may be.

French Kiss

There's no evidence that the French engage in *French-kissing* (inserting one's tongue into another person's mouth) more than any other nationality does. The English language, especially its slang, has a long history (since at least the sixteenth century) of ascribing anything alien, exotic, or risqué to the French, often in a derogatory sense. Thus syphilis was known from the seventeenth century as *the French pox,* condoms were called *French letters,* and even simple swearwords or obscenities were known as *French,* a usage still heard in the phrase *Pardon my French,* meaning "Please excuse my swearing."

French kiss is a much more recent coinage than other *French* terms, having first appeared in the early twentieth century, and rather than reflecting the nationalistic animosity of earlier slurs such as *to take French leave* meaning "to desert," it employs *French* in the sense of "spicy" or "exotic." The same sense of *French* was probably known to your grandfather in the term *French postcards,* slang for erotic photographs current in the early to mid–twentieth century.

There's no evidence that the French engage in FRENCH-KISSING more than any other nationality does.

Gallivant

Gallivant is a fine old word, meaning, in the words of the *Oxford English Dictionary,* "to gad about in a showy fashion, [especially] with persons of the other sex." *To gad* means "to wander around idly," so *gallivanting* translates more or less as "wandering around flirting." The origins of *gallivant* are a bit obscure, although it is almost certainly related to *gallant* as a noun, meaning "ladies' man." The late poet and etymologist John Ciardi suspected that *gallivant* was actually a combination of the French form of *gallant* and *avant* (meaning "forward"), thus giving us "to go out and play the ladies' man."

The late poet and etymologist John Ciardi suspected that GALLIVANT was actually a combination of the French form of GALLANT and AVANT (meaning "forward"), thus giving us "to go out and play the ladies' man."

Get Laid

Many people assume that because *to get laid* and its transitive form, *to lay,* meaning "to have sexual intercourse," are still taboo in many contexts, the terms must be fairly recent inventions. And most dictionaries do date these terms to the early 1930s or even the

1940s. But anyone familiar with the King James Bible of 1611 will recognize *lay* and *laid* simply as forms of the verb *to lie*, which frequently pops up in the Bible and has been used since at least the twelfth century to mean "to have sex." Granted, some uses of *lay* and *lie* found in the Bible, Shakespeare, and other classics are ambiguous, but trust us, when Shakespeare wrote, in *Henry VIII*, "The sly whoresons have got a speeding trick to lay down ladies," he wasn't talking about a Barcalounger.

When Shakespeare wrote, in HENRY VIII, "The sly whoresons have got a speeding trick to lay down ladies," he wasn't talking about a Barcalounger.

Gigolo

A *gigolo* is a kept man, a companion to, and financially supported by, a woman (usually of greater years and always of greater wealth). The archetypal gigolo is a parasite, trading on his good looks, youth, and skill in flattery to earn his living as, essentially, a male prostitute.

Considering that a number of less-than-complimentary terms applied to women (for example, *coquette*) are derived from masculine nouns (in this case, *coq*) that have conveniently fallen into obscurity, it seems only fair that one of the most scathing epithets that can be hurled at a man should have its roots in a feminine noun.

The *gigolette* in French is a dance hall girl (from *giguer,* "to dance," related to the English word *jig*) and, by extension, a prostitute. The masculine form *gigolo* first appeared in English shortly after World War I, and an article in *Women's Home Companion* in 1922 painted a vivid portrait of the creature: "A gigolo, generally speaking, is a man who lives off women's money. In the mad year 1922 . . . a gigolo, definitely speaking, designated one of those incredible and pathetic male creatures, . . . who, for ten francs . . . would dance with any woman wishing to dance . . . in the cafés, hotels, and restaurants of France."

Dancing, of course, is the least of a gigolo's duties, and while use of the term seems to have faded, replaced by trendier (and less pejorative) terms such as *boy toy,* calling a man a *gigolo* (presuming the gigolo understands the term) remains an insult.

Groom

As important as good grooming is to a man about to be married, there is only an indirect connection between *groom,* the verb meaning "to give a tidy appearance to," and *groom* in the wedding sense, which is really a shortened form of *bridegroom.*

Let's begin at the beginning, with *groom* in the "comb your hair" sense. No one has ever been able to figure out exactly where this *groom* came from. It just showed up one day, back when folks were speaking Middle English, and none of the words in other languages that look like *groom* could be proved to be relatives. In any case, this *groom* at first simply meant "young man" or "male servant." But because young male servants were likely to be put to work taking care of horses, the meaning of *groom* shifted over the years to mean "a male servant caring for horses" and then, by extension, "the act of brushing and caring for horses." *Grooming* eventually broadened beyond horses to apply to any sort of hygiene or preparation, such as grooming a candidate for office.

Meanwhile, back at the "bridegroom" kind of *groom,* the original form of this term for the lucky man was *brydguma* (literally, "bride's man"), combining the Old English *bryd,* "bride," with *guma,* "man." Over the years, people stopped using *guma* by itself but were still using the term *brydguma.* Eventually the more familiar *groom* supplanted the by now obsolete *guma,* and *brydguma* eventually became *bridegroom.*

Hanky-Panky

Hanky-panky is a tricky little term that has, appropriately, two separate meanings. When the term first appeared in the mid–nineteenth century, *hanky-panky* meant "trickery" or "devious activity," as in "The congressional subcommittee opened investigations today on hanky-panky in the energy industry." *Hanky-panky* in this sense almost always refers to clandestine corruption in business or political dealings.

But *hanky-panky* is also used to mean "illicit sexual activity," especially in a context where such goings-on would be thought unlikely or considered improper, as within a congressional sub-committee. But no one would be shocked by hanky-panky taking place in a seedy motel, so it wouldn't really be hanky-panky.

Hanky-panky probably arose as a mutation of *hocus-pocus*, the traditional nonsense-word incantation used by magicians while performing a trick, such as making a rabbit disappear. Many people caught in the midst of hanky-panky have probably wished that trick would work on them.

Head over Heels

We all know the signs, and we've seen them in our friends if not in our own mirror. The constant babbling about the beloved. The pathetic attempts to relate every non-beloved-related topic of conversation to the beloved, even if the topic of conversation is deficit spending, local zoning laws, or quantum mechanics. That dreamy glow that makes all attempts at rational conversation pointless.

The question is, why do we say that a person has fallen HEAD OVER HEELS in love with someone when the normal posture of a human being is, in fact, head over heels?

The question is, why do we say that such a person has fallen *head over heels* in love with someone, meaning that the person has figuratively been turned upside down by his or her emotions, when the normal posture of a human being is, in fact, head over heels? The answer is that when the phrase first appeared around 1350, it was in the more logical form *heels over head.* Our garbled modern *head over heels* is the legacy of an apparently badly confused author back in 1771, who wrote, describing a fistfight, "He gave [him] such a violent involuntary kick in the Face, as drove him Head over Heels," and we've been stuck with *head over heels* ever since.

Heartbroken

The course of true love never did run smooth," Shakespeare observed helpfully in *A Midsummer Night's Dream,* but judging from current divorce statistics, that's putting it very mildly. Anybody who has not been disappointed, dejected, crushed, or despondent after the failure or collapse of love simply hasn't been paying attention.

The heart has long been regarded as the home of our nobler emotions such as love (as opposed, for instance, to the spleen, which governs political passions), so when true love tips over the cliff, it makes sense to say, as we have since the sixteenth century, that our heart is "broken," as if the organ itself had been damaged.

It is possible, of course, to be heartbroken over something other than love gone wrong. For instance, many American men would probably be heartbroken if the Superbowl were rained out. Then again, in many cases, only in the wake of such a disaster might these men notice that their wives had left them weeks before.

Hickey

Showing up for work on Monday morning with a hickey may be embarrassing, but at least it doesn't make you a hick. There's no apparent connection between *hickey,* a skin blemish caused by passionate sucking or biting, and *hick,* a derogatory term for an unsophisticated and gullible rural dweller. *Hick* is actually a cropped form of the name *Richard,* which at one time was considered a typically rustic name, much in the same way we got *rube* from the supposedly dorky name *Reuben.*

Hickey, when it first appeared at the beginning of the twentieth century, originally meant simply "small gadget" or "something of no importance," a sense still found in the term *doohickey* (which itself is a melding of *hickey* and *doodad*). *Hickey* and *doodad* (like their synonyms *dingus* and *widget*) are mysterious in origin, probably coined at random as silly words to describe a variety of small, odd objects. At some point around 1918, people started using *hickey* as slang for a pimple or other skin flaw, but it wasn't until the 1940s that *hickey* came to be synonymous with "love bite." Incidentally, short of heavy makeup, there is no quick remedy for the red mark, but it is well known that time heals all hickeys.

Hit On

Anyone who says romance is dead has some pretty powerful evidence in the spread of the phrase *hit on,* meaning "to make romantic advances toward or, especially, to sexually proposition." While the verb *to hit* has been around since at least A.D. 1200 (developed from the Old English *hyttan,* "to meet with"), and figurative uses *(hit upon, hit the bottle)* have been common, *hit on* only became common in the 1960s. As slang for "to make a sexual advance toward," *hit on* is nearly the polar opposite of such venerable terms as *court, romance,* or even the prosaic *date. Hit on* is, in fact, so blunt as to make formerly scandalous terms such as *affair* and *assignation* look refined.

Honeymoon

According to one explanation for *honeymoon* found on the Internet, "It was the accepted practice in Babylonia 4,000 years ago that for a month after the wedding, the bride's father would supply his son-in-law with all the mead he could drink. Mead is a honey beer, and because the Babylonian calendar was lunar-based, this period was called the 'honey month' or what we know today as the 'honeymoon.'"

Nice story, but not even close. Leaving aside the question of why any Babylonian father in his right mind would want his new son-in-law dead drunk for the first month of his daughter's marriage, *honeymoon* first appeared in 1546, a fact that renders Babylonian drinking habits moot.

The most likely explanation of *honeymoon* is the obvious one—that the first month or so of any union is the "sweetest," free of the stresses and strains that later test every marriage. And despite the fact that the period known as a *moon* roughly corresponds to one month, there's no evidence that the *moon* in *honeymoon* has anything to do with the lunar cycle. A more plausible interpretation, first proposed by the lexicographer Samuel Johnson, is that the *moon* in *honeymoon* really refers to the waxing and waning of the moon. In this somewhat cynical scenario, the "moon" of marriage is full at its start, leaving only the natural waning to follow. Of course, any student of lunar affairs knows that the moon always waxes full again, so hope springs eternal.

 There's no evidence that the MOON in HONEYMOON has anything to do with the lunar cycle.

Hook Up

Welcome to the age of vagueness. Back in the early twentieth century, *hook up* was slang for "to meet up with" or "to join," as one might say, "You buy the tickets and I'll hook up with you at the theater." It also meant "to get married," and by the looser 1980s, *hook up* was being used as slang for "become involved in a romantic relationship."

Sometime in the early 1990s, however, college students began using *hook up* as a synonym for (1) "date," (2) "kiss," (3) "neck," and (4) "have sex," thus collapsing the entire mating process into one tepid phrase (which, for many people beyond college age, conjures up all the romantic atmosphere of a tow truck). Oh, well, whatever.

Horny

Every generation of horny teenagers tends to believe that it invented not only sexual slang but sex itself. Actually, *horny,* meaning "sexually excited," dates back to at least the early nineteenth century, and *horn* as euphemistic slang for "erect penis" dates back to the fifteenth century (although women as well as men can now be described as horny). Shakespeare even used *horn* in this sense to make a pun in *The Taming of the Shrew* (circa 1594) and got away with it.

The choice of *horn* as a euphemism was not random. Horns have been considered symbols of fertility since ancient times, as have horned animals such as bulls, stags, and goats, and the ancient belief that powdered horn is an aphrodisiac persists in many cultures.

Hug

Hugging is perhaps the most universal display of affection among human beings. *To hug* means "to squeeze or clasp a person in one's arms, usually as a show of love or affection."

Although people have been hugging one another since the dawn of history, the English word *hug* is a surprisingly recent arrival, having first appeared less than five hundred years ago. We probably borrowed our *hug* from one of the Scandinavian languages, most probably from the Old Norse verb *hugga,* meaning "to comfort, console, protect."

Hunk

Elvis Presley's hit rendition of Dennis Linde's song "Burning Love," with its refrain "hunkahunka burning love," may have given *hunk* a big boost as popular slang for "a muscular and very attractive man," but it definitely didn't invent the usage. *Hunk,* from the Flemish *hunke,* meaning "lump," is a relatively recent arrival in our language, having first appeared in the early nineteenth century with the meaning "a thick chunk or piece of something," as in "a hunk of bread." By the late nineteenth century, *hunk* was slang for "a large, slow, and somewhat stupid man." In the 1940s, *hunk* became slang for "an especially attractive person, either male or female," but by the 1970s, hunks, possibly reflecting the omnipresent Presley hit, were exclusively male, and they have been ever since.

Husband

Husband is what is termed a *correlative* of the word *wife*, which is to say that each is defined in relation to the other. Without a *wife* there would be no *husband*, and without a husband there would be talk among the neighbors. This is why the most important words in married life are *Where have you been?*

The interesting thing about *husband* is how long it took to show up in its modern sense. One of the Old English words for "man" was *were*, now found only in one common English word, *werewolf*. But we also borrowed the word *husbondi* from Old Norse, which meant literally "house dweller" and was used in English in the sense of "master of the house" with no particular marital status implied. This "guy in charge" meaning of

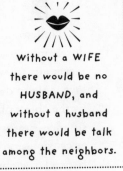

Without a WIFE there would be no HUSBAND, and without a husband there would be talk among the neighbors.

husband persists today in the verb *to husband,* meaning "to cultivate or manage," as well as in terms such as *animal husbandry,* for "the raising and care of livestock" (which leads in turn to the old Tom Lehrer line about the student who majored in animal husbandry until they caught him at it).

But while *husband* had been part of the language since Old English times, the modern meaning of "a man married to a woman" only appeared in the thirteenth century, by which time the matching term *wife* had been impatiently tapping its toe for nearly five hundred years.

Infatuation

To be *infatuated* is to find oneself, often quite suddenly and for no logical reason, utterly, obsessively in love with someone or something.

Hollywood is in love with romantic infatuation. At least a dozen movies are produced every year on the theme of boy meets girl (or vice versa) and goes completely bonkers with love, only to discover that his (or her) feelings are not shared by the object of his (or her) passion. But through dogged persistence, bravery, cleverness, and often a car chase and a few large explosions, he (or she) wins his (or her) beloved in the last reel, thereby proving that what had seemed to be an irrational obsession was actually *true love,* which, of course, always wins out.

In real life, of course, this kind of infatuation often leads at best to bitter disappointment, a fate foretold by the origin of the word itself. *Infatuare* is a Latin verb meaning "to make foolish," related to our modern word *fatuous*. When *infatuate* first appeared in English in the sixteenth century, it meant "to make to look foolish; to embarrass; to frustrate," in the sense that one might endeavor to *infatuate* one's opponent in a debate. Popular manias or fads were also said to infatuate the public with foolish enthusiasm, precursors of our current infatuation with the computer.

Jealousy

Jealousy is a very old word with a number of meanings, so we'd better start off by narrowing things down a bit. We're not talking about *jealousy* in the "envy" sense of begrudging a billionaire his yachts, or a rock star his fame or fans. We're not talking about *jealousy* in the "protective anxiety" sense, as a child jealously guards his sand castle from vandals. We're not even talking about the biblical sort of *jealousy*, the Judeo-Christian God's legendary intolerance of competition.

Since JEALOUSY inspires the zealous, it's appropriate that JEALOUSY comes from the Greek word ZELOS.

No, we're talking about the "examining your spouse's credit card receipts and cell phone bills" kind of *jealousy*. The "hiding in the shrubbery outside your lover's apartment building" kind of *jealousy*. The "keep that up and I'm gonna get a restraining order" kind of *jealousy*. In this sense, *jealousy* is defined by the *Oxford English Dictionary* as "the state of mind arising from the suspicion, apprehension, or knowledge of rivalry," but it is usually known to its practitioners and their defense attorneys as *true love*.

Since jealousy inspires the zealous (and often overzealous) safeguarding of the beloved's beloving, it's appropriate that *jealousy* comes from the Greek word *zelos*. In addition to simple "jealousy," *zelos* also meant "enthusiasm" or "fervor" and is the root of our modern *zealous* and *zealot*.

Jealousy has always been a word that echoed the ambivalence of the emotion itself. When *jealousy* first appeared in English in the fifteenth century, it meant both "vehemence of feeling *for* a person" and "vehemence of feeling *against* a person."

Jilt

One sad truth about human relationships is that love is, more often than not, a zero-sum game. The unilateral subtraction of one lover (also known as *dumping*), though frequently ascribed to boredom, incompatibility, or that annoying habit he has of sucking his teeth, is often eerily coincident with the arrival of a new love interest. Quite often, in fact, the old familiar hasn't a clue that a new ship has even appeared on the horizon until the newcomer has been greeted with a brass band and garlands of flowers and is well into the process of docking.

While the joyous dockee invariably refers to this process of jettisoning yesterday's beloved as *growing* or *turning the page* or similar psychobabble, the sad sap left on the previous page knows full well that he has been jilted.

To jilt means to be "false or faithless in love," to "trick, delude, or hold out false hopes in love," or "to discard one lover for another." *Jilt* first appeared in English in

If a specific woman named Gillian way back then inspired all this, whoever she jilted certainly got his revenge.

the late seventeenth century, although the practice itself is obviously much older. A clue to the origin of *jilt* may be found in the fact that *jilt* started out as a noun meaning "faithless woman" or "harlot" and is possibly related to the earlier term *gillot* (or *gill*), a disparaging term for a woman, roughly equivalent to "wench." *Gill*, in turn, is simply an abbreviated form of the female name *Gillian*. And if a specific woman named Gillian way back then inspired all this, whoever she jilted certainly got his revenge.

Kiss

Though a simple gesture, a kiss can carry a multitude of meanings. The parent's kiss is an entirely different creature from the lover's kiss, and an innocent child's kiss hardly seems the same act as the sort of kiss-before-whacking that is a fixture of gangster movies. But even the most inane kiss can have consequences: to sidestep the empty *air-kissing* of Hollywood may mean the *kiss of death* for an actor's career.

Strictly speaking, according to the *Oxford English Dictionary, to kiss* means "to press or touch with the lips (at the same time compressing and then separating them), in token of affection or greeting, or as an act of reverence; to salute or caress with the lips. . . ." Figuratively, any light contact between two things (billiard balls, car bumpers, moonlight and a damsel's hair, and so forth) can be described as a *kiss.*

Kiss is a very old word, so old in fact that its ultimate source is obscured by the mists of time (that is, no one has a clue). The English word *kiss,* which developed from Old English around A.D. 750, has numerous relatives in other Germanic languages (for example, the Dutch word *kussen* and the Danish *kysse*). In all likelihood, the origin of *kiss* in prehistoric times was what linguists call *echoic,* meaning that the word arose as an imitation of the sound of the act of kissing itself.

Lascivious

ascivious is a fine old word, having first appeared in English around 1450. Unfortunately, *lascivious* is used too rarely today and is usually encountered only in court proceedings or newspaper accounts striving to render the unprintable printable.

Although the basic definition of *lascivious* is "inclined to lust; engaging in lewd or wanton behavior," *lascivious* is not, at heart, a tawdry word. The root of *lascivious* is the Latin *lascivus,* which meant "playful" or "sportive." *Lascivious* is a good-natured word, fun to pronounce ("lah-SIV-ee-ous"), and almost impossible to say with a straight face.

LASCIVIOUS is not, at heart, a tawdry word.

Lecher

A*lecher* isn't just a pushy party animal. He's the loser with the Playboy Bunny decal on his car, the connoisseur of gold chains and garish sunglasses, the self-proclaimed swinger whose idea of scintillating conversation inevitably begins with "Hey, baby." The lecher actually looks forward to all the porno spam he gets. The lecher is a dirty old man in training.

The lecher is a dirty old man in training.

The origin of *lecher* (often shortened simply to *lech*) reinforces the word's connotations of seediness and smarm. *Lecher* was imported into English in the thirteenth century from the Old French *lecheor,* which meant literally "one who licks" and figuratively "one who lives a life of dissolute pleasure." The connection with licking is probably due to the fact that the original sense of *lecher* included gluttony as one of the degenerate practices of a lecher.

Lewd

Lewd, which today means "lustful" or "obscene," is a good example of how a word can change meanings over the centuries. Back in the twelfth century, when *lewd* was spelled *lewed* (from the Old English *laewede*), the word meant simply "a lay person, not a member of the clergy." Since the clergy at that time encompassed most of the literate members of society, *lewd* was also a synonym for "illiterate," or "uneducated." And since the lower, uneducated sectors of society were considered ill-mannered and unrefined, *lewd* came to mean "vulgar" and, by extension, "sinful," "vile," and "evil." By the fourteenth century, *lewd* had attained its modern meaning of "sexually suggestive," "salacious," or "obscene." In the twentieth century, *lewd* enjoyed the spotlight in public debates over the definition of pornography (the phrase *lewd and lascivious* is frequently found in court decisions), but with the advent of such distinctions as *hard-core* and *soft-core* porn, the simple *lewd* may be headed for oblivion.

Liaison

When the plot thickens, and not just any euphemism will do, say it in French. With luck, your listeners will be so impressed (or appalled) by your pronunciation that they'll miss the implications of what you're saying. And if you're writing, they'll be wondering if you spelled it correctly.

When *liaison* (taken directly from the French, originally

from the Latin *ligare,* meaning "to bind") first appeared in English in the sixteenth century, it was, strangely enough, as a cooking term. A *liaison* was an ingredient, most often egg yolks, added to thicken sauce or gravy and to bind the ingredients together.

A *LIAISON* was an ingredient, most often egg yolks, added to thicken sauce or gravy and to bind the ingredients together.

The general sense of "something that binds" led, in the early eighteenth century, to the use of *liaison* to mean "any sort of close and often clandestine relationship between two parties," be they people, businesses, or even countries, as in the secret liaisons rumored between certain European powers in the great geopolitical game of empire building.

Between people, however, *liaison* soon took on the meaning of "illicit intimacy," making *liaison* a high-class euphemism for "affair."

Libertine

Today we use *libertine* to mean "a person who blatantly flouts society's generally accepted rules of moral conduct, especially regarding sexual behavior." Hugh Hefner, the publisher of *Playboy,* was for many decades regarded as America's leading libertine, a title now made irrelevant by any weekday's crop of guests on the *Jerry Springer Show* and its kind.

But while *libertine* may be out of a job at the moment, the history of the word is an interesting historical tour of what our

Hugh Hefner was for many decades regarded as America's leading libertine.

society has regarded, at various times, as being "free" (and sometimes "too free"). When *libertine* first appeared in English around 1382, derived from the Latin *libertus* (meaning "freed"), it was applied in historical accounts to Roman slaves who had been freed from bondage. By the sixteenth century, a *libertine* was a freethinker in matters of religion, and the term held much the same weight of condemnation as *apostate* or *infidel.* By the seventeenth century, *libertine* had been secularized and was used to describe anyone who disregarded the conventions of art, literature, or society in general. Then, as simple social nonconformity lost its shock value, *libertine* took on the more restricted sense of "a sexually promiscuous, dissolute person who is willing to break any social taboo in pursuit of his or her pleasure."

Long

So, if *to long for* means "to deeply desire someone or something," being utterly indifferent to the subject must be *to short for* it?

Not quite, but the verb *to long* is indeed essentially the same word as the familiar adjective *long,* meaning "possessing substantial length." As you might expect, a useful word like the adjective *long* goes way back—in this case, at least all the way back to the Latin *longus,* meaning (what else?) "long." Our English *long* has very similar relatives in German, Dutch, Danish, Italian, French, and several other languages —just about everywhere you'd find a tape measure in western Europe has some form of *long*.

As a verb, *to long* developed separately from the adjective in Old English and first appeared in English around A.D. 1000, when it meant, quite logically, "to make longer," either physically or in duration (both of which senses are now handled by the related *lengthen*). The "yearning" sense of *to long,* which developed around 1300, reflects the idea of something or someone being a long way away or taking a long time to arrive. One can easily imagine the wife of a sea captain, for instance, longing for the return of her husband from distant lands. The phrase *to long away,* meaning "to put far away" or "to depart," was in use during the same period and also reflected the fact that in the days when rapid transit was a donkey cart, distance often equaled near oblivion. Today, in the era of jet travel and instant gratification, we perhaps spend less time longing for people and things to arrive, but *longing* still lives in the hearts of unrequited lovers waiting for that certain someone to metaphorically come around.

Lothario

Lothario is evidence that some things, and some types of people, never change. A *Lothario* is a love-'em-and-leave-'em Casanova, a frivolous seducer, and (need we say it?) an untrustworthy cad. *Lothario* is an *eponym,* a word formed from the proper name of a famous real

The original LOTHARIO was a character in Nicholas Rowe's 1703 play THE FAIR PENITENT.

or fictional person. The original *Lothario* was a character in Nicholas Rowe's 1703 play *The Fair Penitent*. Rowe (1674–1718) was famous for his "she-tragedies," the eighteenth-century theatrical equivalent of today's "weepy" movies, such as *Terms of Endearment*. In Rowe's play, the heroine, Calista, is first seduced and then, inevitably, abandoned by the "gallant, gay Lothario" (*gay* meaning "loose" or "immoral" at the time). Calista, in keeping with the conventions of the genre, commits suicide, leaving *Lothario* to become a synonym for the sort of man women should avoid more often than they do.

Love

Writers, poets, and philosophers have been trying to define *love* since the dawn of civilization, with limited success, but the *Oxford English Dictionary* definition, while not very romantic (especially in its use of the term *object*), hits most of the high points: "That disposition or state of feeling with regard to a person which (arising from recognition of attractive qualities, from instincts of natural relationship, or from sympathy) manifests itself in solicitude for the welfare of the object, and usually also in delight in his or her presence and desire for his or her approval; warm affection, attachment."

We inherited the word *love* from Old English, but its root

is much older: the Indo-European root *leubh*. How old is old? The asterisk (*) preceding *leubh* means that the word itself has not actually been found in ancient sources but is inferred by linguists from subsequent word formations. In addition to *love,* that ancient *leubh* produced the equivalent words for *love* in a number of European languages (for example, *liebe* in German), as well as the Latin *libido* and even the English *belief.*

Lovelorn

According to legend, the nightingale sings her late-night song because of a broken heart. Ornithologists, however, point out that if every nightingale were suffering from lost love, there wouldn't be any nightingales around in the first place. But a glance at the personal-advice columns in today's newspapers proves that plenty of *lovelorn* human beings are singing the lovesick blues.

Lovelorn is a slightly antiquated word meaning "forsaken by one's beloved" or "pining for a lost love." The poet John Milton was apparently the first author to use *love-lorn,* in 1634, but the adjective *lorn* had already been in use for more than three centuries. *Lorn* is actually just a past participle of the obsolete verb *leese,* an early form of our modern *lose.* So *lovelorn* simply amounts to "love lost."

While the song of the nightingale is certainly haunting and sad, the legend of

The poet John Milton apparently was the first author to use LOVE-LORN, in 1634.

Gimme an L

Love is all you need," sang the Beatles, and while that may not, strictly speaking, be true, the word *love* itself has indeed spawned a varied range of words and phrases. Here are a few of the more common *love* coinages.

Love Apple: A sixteenth-century term for a tomato. Probably a literal translation of the French *pomme d'amour,* reflecting the belief, common at the time, that tomatoes are an aphrodisiac. Today we know that this is only true if they are baked into a pizza.

Love Beads: A necklace of colorful beads worn by hippies in the 1960s as a symbol of love and peace. Went out of fashion when the beads proved to be too convenient a handle used by arresting officers.

Lovebirds: Small birds, usually parrots of the genus *Agapornis,* kept as pets and noted for their affectionate behavior toward their mate. Human lovebirds are also known for their effusive public displays of affection, though cynics point out that the birds mate for life, a practice considerably rarer in the human lovebird.

Love Child: A nineteenth-century euphemism for a child born outside of marriage, gentle by comparison to the alternatives used at various times: *bastard, natural child, child born on the wrong side of the blanket,* *by-child,* the clever but nasty *sinfant,* and the equine metaphor *wood colt* (an analogy to a horse sired by an unknown stallion in the woods).

Love Feast: Originally a meal shared by early Christians to spread feelings of goodwill. Now usually used in a sarcastic sense to describe an occasion of fulsome admiration ("The president's press conference was turned into a love feast by a mesmerized press corps").

Love Handles: From the 1970s, deposits of fat on the sides of the waist. A seemingly affectionate term that in fact usually denotes subtle disapproval.

Love-In: A 1960s gathering of hippies intended to transform the world by radiating mass quantities of good vibes. Did not work.

Lovesick: From the sixteenth century, suffering grievously from either too much or too little love. If love were within the purview of the FDA, it would have been taken off the market years ago.

Loveseat: A small sofa with room for just two people. Some older loveseats were designed to facilitate amorous conversation by seating the couple facing each other, but these disappeared with the advent of television.

Loving Cup: From the nineteenth century, a large vessel with ornate handles, filled with wine and passed among guests as a sign of mutual affection at the conclusion of a banquet. Now usually seen as the trophy presented to the winner of a competition that involves anything but mutual affection.

the little bird's broken heart may have much to do with the fact
that *lovelorn* humans are the most likely of their species to sit
up late at night listening to birds.

Lust

It's a noun. It's a verb. For some people, it's a lifestyle.
It's *lust,* and although, when it first entered Old English from its Germanic roots, *lust* meant simply
"pleasure" or "appetite," for most of its history *lust* has meant
just what it means today: "sexual desire." In comparison to such
refined synonyms as *desire, ardor,* or *passion,* however, *lust* has
always carried a nasty hint of the heavy-breathing animal in all
of us, making it a natural choice for number one among the
Seven Deadly Sins.

Today, however, we live in a commercial age where lust is
often invoked as an impetus not to procreate but to purchase,
with the shopping mall replacing the boudoir as the locus of
passion and "My place or yours?" being supplanted by "Visa or
MasterCard?"

Macho

Here's a strange coincidence: the first definition of
macho listed in the *Oxford English Dictionary* is
"the California mullet," a species of fish. *Mullet*
is also the name of a type of haircut (short on top, very long in

back) favored by men who, generally speaking, would also be described as *macho* in the more common sense of "aggressively masculine."

The connections, if any, among the fish, the haircut, and a tendency to flex one's biceps as a rhetorical device are a bit hazy, but *macho* (from the Mexican Spanish vernacular *macho*, meaning "male animal") first entered English in the 1920s as slang for "a tough guy." By the time the feminist movement got rolling in the late 1960s, *macho* had entered common usage as a pejorative adjective meaning "ostentatiously manly or virile," often modifying the noun *pig*.

Mash

In love, as in potatoes, there can be too much of a good thing. At least that's the apparent lesson of the curious word *mash*.

To mash, in the standard sense, means "to crush, pound, or beat to a pulp in order to soften," as one does when preparing mashed potatoes. The ultimate root of *mash* was the Old English *masc,* meaning "the soft malt or grain-meal mixture used as a starting point for brewing beer."

However, in the late nineteenth century, *mash* appeared in the United States both as a slang noun meaning "an infatuation," and a verb meaning "to flirt or to make romantic advances." Soon young folks besotted by love were sending *mash notes*—short romantic letters—to the objects of their affections. All was not sweetness and light, however. A young man who pressed his

In love, as in potatoes, there can be too much of a good thing. At least that's the apparent lesson of the curious word MASH.

attentions on a young woman who was not interested came to be known as a *masher*, a pejorative term still in use today.

The connection between crushing potatoes and sparking romance is not immediately obvious, and the logic of *mash* in the slang sense is the subject of much debate. The most logical assumption is that *to mash* in the romantic sense is to concentrate one's attentions on the beloved in hopes of "softening" his or her heart.

One indication that the story may be a bit more complicated is that *mash* may well have originated in the slang of the theater in the late nineteenth century, where for an actor *to mash* meant to "ham it up" by smiling or flirting with one or more audience members while onstage. Such opportunistic antics lend credence to the theory that the English *mash* was borrowed from the Romany (the language of the Gypsies, of which there were many in the English theater at that time). In Romany, *mash* means "to entice or delude," a definition that certainly fits both the behavior of manipulative actors and a cynical view of romance.

Mate

Moonlight, music, romance—bah, humbug! It's all about food. Etymologically, a *mate* is someone you'd be willing to share your sandwich with. The Germanic root of *mate* was *gamaton,* formed from the prefix *ga,* "together," plus *mat,* which also gave us the word *meat.* So the original sense of *mate,* which arrived in English around 1380, was "someone you eat with or share your food with; a friend or companion." (A *companion,* in fact, was also originally someone who shared your food, from the Latin *com,* meaning "together," plus *panis,* meaning "bread").

And although we now tend to associate *mate* with love, marriage, and sex (as in, for example, the phrase *mating rituals*), the primary meaning of *mate* throughout most of its history has been "friend," "comrade," or "partner," later taking on the meaning of "assistant," as in the *surgeon's mate* aboard ship. The sense of *mate* meaning "a partner in marriage" (or simply "a lover") didn't arise until the mid–sixteenth century, about the same time that *mate* took on the meaning of "one of a matched pair of things" by analogy to a mated pair of humans. So, strictly speaking, human beings haven't been mating any longer than sweat socks have.

Matrimony

One might suspect that *matrimony,* the act of two people joining in marriage, or the state of those people after such joining, is related to the word *mate.* But that would make perfect sense, which would mean that *matrimony* would violate what seems to be commandment numero uno of the English language: Thy words shalt make little, if any, sense.

So *matrimony,* which English inherited from the Latin *matrimonium* in the fourteenth century, has nothing to do with *mate. Matrimony* is based on *matri,* a form of the Latin *mater,* meaning "mother," also found in such words as *matrilineal, matriarch,* and *matricide.* (The suffix *mony* doesn't really mean anything beyond "a state of being.") Of course, anyone who needs to ask what marriage has to do with mothers has either never been married or is married and lacks a telephone. Strangely enough, though, *matrimony,* in a curious reversal of its roots, really has nothing to do with mothers. Instead, the *matri* in *matrimony* refers to women in general, so etymologically, *matrimony* really means just "the state of being related or bound to a woman." And, naturally, to her mother.

Monogamy

As if "until death do us part" weren't strict enough. The original meaning of *monogamy* wasn't its modern meaning of "being married to, and faithful to, one person at a time" (much less its extended common meaning of "remaining faithful to one person during a sexual relationship outside of marriage").

No, when *monogamy* first appeared in English around 1612, it meant "the practice of marrying only once" and specifically "not remarrying after the death of a spouse." If you were going to be monogamous back then, you got exactly one shot at marriage, and (especially given the substantially lower life expectancy in those days) you'd better hope you'd picked a healthy mate. Marrying another person after the demise of the first spouse was known as *digamy*, and it was frowned on in some social circles.

By the early eighteenth century, *monogamy* (from the Greek *mono*, "one," plus *gamy*, "marriage") had lightened up to mean just "one spouse at a time." Of course, being married to two folks at the same time (*bigamy*, from the Greek *bi*, or "two"), or possessing a platoon of mates (*polygamy*, from the Greek *poly*, "many"), were then and still are considered crimes in many jurisdictions.

In a measure of how far social and sexual standards have loosened over the centuries, a recent invention in the taxonomy of *monogamy* is *serial monogamy*, meaning "sexual fidelity to one person during the course of a relationship that is acknowledged to be unlikely to last," also known as *until someone new entering the room do us part*.

Moonstruck

Moonlight becomes you, I'm thrilled at the sight / And I could get so romantic tonight," crooned Bing Crosby in the classic Crosby–Hope movie *The Road to Morocco* in 1942, and the Johnny Burke and Jimmy Van Heusen song "Moonlight Becomes You" shot to the top of the charts.

But for much of human history, the going wisdom was more like "Moonlight drives you nuts." Exposure to the light of the moon, especially the full moon, was believed to cause a wide range of unpleasant mental symptoms, ranging from moodiness to outright insanity. (The full moon was also, of course, known to rile up werewolves and witches.)

So firm was the popular belief in the harmful powers of moonlight that even today we speak colloquially of the deranged as *lunatics,* a thirteenth-century term drawn from the Latin word for "moon," *luna.* The term *moonstruck,* which first appeared in the seventeenth century, started out meaning roughly the same thing as *lunatic*—that the person had been struck or stunned, scrambled, confused, and maddened by exposure to the full moon. The moonstruck victim could even, it was said, exhibit dire physical symptoms, such as blindness, whenever the moon was full.

But perhaps because fear of the moon and its light were waning by the nineteenth century, *moonstruck* lost its alarming connotations and came to describe someone who is mildly addled, dazed, and confused not by the moon but by a romantic infatuation.

Mushy

As amazing as it may seem, *mush* has its partisans. Real *mush,* a porridge made from cornmeal boiled in water or milk, is a staple of breakfast in many parts of the United States, and is usually served in a bowl with butter and milk but may also be fried. *Mush* is an example of an onomatopoeic coinage: the word itself sounds like something soft, wet, and easily digestible.

Mush first appeared in English back in the seventeenth century, and by the early nineteenth century both *mush* and *mushy* were being used to describe anything soft and squishy. By the late nineteenth century, *mushy* was being used as a derogatory term to describe anything considered insipidly emotional, cloyingly sweet, or sappy: "They formed a circle around Sally and Peter and as mushy as ever they could they sang, 'As sure as the grass grows around the stump, You are my darling sugar lump,' while they danced" (G. S. Porter, *Laddie* [1913]).

Mush, of course, is in the eye of the beholder. One might well argue that if vast numbers of consumers didn't love tear-jerkers, "very special" episodes of sitcoms, and romance novels, they wouldn't exist to be disparaged.

Necking

Some things never change, although the terminology certainly does. Dictionaries have not yet labeled *necking* (which first appeared around 1825) "antiquated" or "obsolete," but the chances of hearing anyone under the age of twenty-one use the term are becoming increasingly slim with every passing year. So maybe it's time to point out that the term *necking* never made much sense to begin with.

The definition of *to neck* offered by the *Oxford English Dictionary,* "to clasp (a member of the opposite sex) round the neck; to fondle," sounds more like a wrestling hold than an expression of affection. Used in an intransitive sense, says the

OED, neck means "to engage in holding and fondling, or to embrace and caress, a member of the opposite sex," a definition that, while it doesn't specifically mention necks, leaves open the disturbing vision of the loving couple grasping each other gently by the throat.

In reality, of course, *necking* has always primarily meant "prolonged passionate kissing," and as such it is one in a long line of euphemisms that includes such fool-nobody classics as *to sleep with.*

Nosegay

A nosegay is a small, sweet-smelling bouquet of flowers, usually gathered by one lover for another on the spur of the moment on a romantic picnic or some other bucolic expedition. A nosegay is not, in other words, ordered from the florist at the mall with your corporate credit card, and a nosegay does not get you frequent-flier miles. A nosegay is the botanic embodiment of a romantic impulse.

The origin of *nosegay,* which first appeared in English in the fifteenth century, is an etymological no-brainer: the fragrance of the flowers makes the recipient's nose gay. The word *gay* in *nosegay* is used in its original sense of "full of mirth and joy; happy, merry, carefree"; an adaptation of the French *gai,* it is possibly connected to a Germanic root meaning "pretty."

Nosegay is less frequently heard today than it once was, almost certainly because the word *gay* is now usually used to mean "homosexual." Grumbling among self-appointed language purists over this supposed hijacking of *gay* was common in the late twentieth century (and is still occasionally heard today), but the use of *gay* to mean things other than "happy" is far from new. In the seventeenth century, *gay* was used to mean "addicted to pleasure," or "self-indulgent" and was applied to anyone, of whatever sexual orientation, who led a life considered immoral or licentious by the arbiters of social morality. Beginning in the early nineteenth century, *gay* had become a euphemism for "engaging in prostitution." The sense of *gay* meaning "homosexual" did not arise until the 1920s.

During the entire three hundred years that *gay* bore the stigma of social ostracism in these senses, however, it was still commonly used in its original "happy and carefree" sense with no apparent problem. Only with the rise of the gay liberation movement in the late 1960s did *gay* develop the apparently embarrassing ambiguity to many people that restricts its use today.

Obsession

I f you were *obsessed* back in the sixteenth century, it meant that your enemies had surrounded your castle and wouldn't let you out (from the Latin *ob* plus *sedere,* meaning "to sit in front of; to block"). Today, a romantic *obsession* means your heart is held prisoner and your beloved won't lower the drawbridge. Romantic obsession has gotten a

If you were **OBSESSED** back in the sixteenth century, it meant that your enemies had surrounded your castle and wouldn't let you out.

Say It with Snapdragons

Flowers have spoken to me more than I can tell in written words. They are the hieroglyphics of angels, loved by all men for the beauty of the character, though few can decipher even fragments of their meaning. —Lydia M. Child

It may be impossible to decode the ultimate meaning of flowers, but that hasn't stopped people from using them to convey their own emotions. From the earliest recorded history, flowers have been dispatched as messengers to express love, loss, fear, regret, and sorrow. For clandestine lovers, flowers have often been used to communicate when a letter or an actual rendezvous would pose the risk of exposure. A bouquet of flowers, a seemingly innocent gesture, could, through the blossoms it contained and their arrangement, convey a multitude of meanings, from an expression of interest, to a desire to meet, to a sad farewell.

Floriography, the modern language of flowers, got its start in 1818, when a certain Charlotte de La Tour wrote *Le Langage des Fleurs,* a sort of decoder ring for amorous botanists that spelled out exactly how to communicate complex emotions in a simple bouquet. Floriography became immensely popular in Victorian England, with dozens of books adding interpretations of the more obscure flowers and expanding the vocabulary of floral giving into a virtual cryptography of leafy correspondence. Even the ribbon used to tie a bouquet carried meaning among the knowledgeable: if tied to the right, the emotions expressed by the blooms referred to

the giver; to the left, to the recipient. The import of a gift of flowers could, of course, be fine-tuned by adding various sprigs of fern or herbs. And if the flowers were presented in person, even the hand used had meaning: the right meant yes; the left, no (possibly, a cynic would say, because the right hand would be needed to fend off the disappointed recipient).

Interestingly, the meanings assigned to particular flowers in floriography usually have little or nothing to do with the names of the flowers or their origins. But while the meanings assigned to flowers in floriography are essentially arbitrary, so, one might say, is all human language. A more practical problem with floriography is the assignment of multiple (and sometimes contradictory) meanings to some flowers, not to mention the variations in meanings given by competing flower dictionaries. One wonders how many Victorian affairs went astray because of floral translation disputes ("No, no, forsythia means 'anticipation,' not 'good-bye forever'!").

While some of the more arcane precepts of floriography have faded in the age of E-mail, many are still commonly accepted by flower lovers. So if you have something to say to that special someone, but the cat's got your tongue (or your computer is clogged with cat fur), study this handy guide to the origins of the names, and the secret meanings, of some popular blossoms, and let a thousand (or at least a dozen) flowers do the talking.

FLOWER NAME	ORIGIN	MESSAGE(S)
Carnation	Probably a variation of **coronation,** reflecting its use in ceremonial crowns in ancient Greece.	Red: Admiration. White: Pure love. Pink: "I will remember you."
Chrysanthemum	From the Greek *chrysos anthos,* meaning "gold flower."	Red: "I love you." White: Truth.
Daffodil	A variation on *affodil* (for "asphodel"), itself a garbled form of that flower's genus, *Asphodelus,* although what we call *daffodils* today belong to the genus *Narcissus.*	Regard; unrequited love; "You're the only one."
Daisy	Old English *daegeseage,* or "day's eye," from the opening and closing of the flower as the sun rises and sets each day.	Innocence.
Forget-Me-Not	Translation of the German *vergiss mein nicht,* fabled farewell cry of a German knight who tossed a bouquet of these to his lady love as he drowned.	True love; memories; "Forget me not."
Hyacinth	From *Hyacinthus,* dear friend of Apollo in Greek mythology, killed by a errant discus thrown by Apollo. The flower is said to have sprung from Hyacinthus's head as he died, and always bends toward the ground as if in grief.	"Forgive me."
Hydrangea	Greek *hydro,* "water," and *aggeion,* "vessel."	Heartlessness.

FLOWER NAME	ORIGIN	MESSAGE(S)
Iris	In Greek mythology, the messenger of the gods, often depicted as a rainbow.	Faith; hope; or a signal that a message is being sent.
Jonquil	From the Latin *junkus*, "rush," for its rushlike leaves	"Your affection is returned."
Peony	From *Paeon*, physician to the gods in Greek mythology, changed into a plant by Zeus.	Shame; bashful love.
Phlox	Greek *phlox*, meaning "flame."	"Our souls are united."
Poppy	From its Latin name, *papaver*, possibly connected to *pap*, milky food resembling the plant's juice.	Eternal sleep; oblivion.
Rose	*Rosa*, Latin for "red."	Pink: Happiness. White: Innocence. Red: Desire; passion.
Snapdragon	Squeezing the sides of the flower will open and close its tip, resembling a dragon's mouth.	Deception; presumption.
Sweet Pea	Member of the pea family with a sweet smell, but not edible.	Departure; "Good-bye."
Tulip	From the Turkish *tuliband*, derived from Persian *dulband*, meaning "turban," which the flower was thought to resemble.	"You are the perfect lover."

bad rap in recent years, and the ex who won't take no for an answer, and maintains an amorous obsession in the face of rejection, ejection, and injunction, has become our modern bogeyman. Still, to be fair, isn't someone who is obsessed really just a "love workaholic?"

Ogle

OGLE comes from the Dutch word OOG, meaning "eye," which is where it all starts but rarely stops.

You're not exactly staring (which is rude), certainly not leering (that's too lewd); you're past the point of eyeing, but not yet up to trying. You're *ogling* that person, aren't you? *Ogle,* which means "to cast amorous glances" and first appeared in English in the seventeenth century, comes from the Dutch word *oog,* meaning "eye," which is where it all starts but rarely stops.

Paramour

It's a good thing we're allowed to use words without being able to explain where they originally came from, because otherwise, the convoluted history of *paramour* would have consigned it to oblivion several centuries ago.

One the surface, *paramour* could hardly be simpler: *par amour* is French for "by [or through] love." When *par amour* first entered English in the thirteenth century, it was as an adverbial phrase meaning "for love's sake," the sort of thing you'd drop into a sentence in the same way we might use *if you please* or *as a favor* (as in "Reggie, par amour, kindly stop sucking your teeth"). Oddly enough, at about the same time, the verb phrase *to love par amour* meant "to love sexually, as a lover."

Par amour, the adverb, then gradually became the noun *paramour,* but it remained more than a little ambiguous. On the one hand, it meant "sweetheart," with connotations of youth, innocence, and purity. It also, however, was used to mean "sexual love," "lover," or "love affair." In a somewhat bizarre side trip, *paramour* was even used in religious texts and hymns as a form of address for both Jesus and the Virgin Mary.

By about the end of the fourteenth century, *paramour* had settled down to mean "lover," especially a partner in an illicit or clandestine affair, but today *paramour* is most often used in a facetious or sarcastic sense (as in "Heather, please ask your paramour not to spit tobacco juice on the porch").

Peccadillo

It may be a fact of life that there's no such thing as being "a little bit pregnant," but almost every other aspect of the human condition is measured in shades of gray. Take the classic Christian theological spectrum of sin, for instance. You've got your seven *mortal sins* (pride, covetousness, lust, envy, gluttony, anger, and liking Billy Joel), any one of which will get you seriously toasted when it comes time to

The Eyes Have It

According to the French poet Guillaume de Salluste Du Bartas (1544–90), the eyes are "the windows of the soul." Whether one can actually see into, let alone reliably judge, the soul of another person through his or her eyes is debatable, but eyes have always played a big part in love. Even today, both the enhancement (eye shadow, colored contact lenses) and the concealment (designer sunglasses) of our eyes are booming industries, and eye-lift plastic surgery is increasingly popular.

But what one *does* with one's eyes is still more important than how one accessorizes them, as witnessed by these venerable ocular inventions.

Sheep's Eyes: When we cast *sheep's eyes* at someone, we are looking at them with yearning and adoration. The origin of this phrase, which appeared in the sixteenth century, is a bit of a mystery, since sheep are not known to be especially romantic creatures, and the average sheep's expression is actually more of a blank stare. Then again, baby sheep come from somewhere, so maybe sheep are onto something.

Leer: *Leer* entered English in about A.D. 700 from the Old Norse word *Hlyr* and originally meant simply "cheek" or "face." At first, *leer* didn't have any of its modern seedy connotations, and to say someone had "a lovely leer" was just another way of saying that they were "pretty" or "cute." Along about the sixteenth century, *leer* came to mean "a sideways glance" (probably because such a glance is done across the cheek) and as a verb, originally meant "to look at something or someone with suspicion." From there it mutated into its current meaning of "a sly or lascivious smile or look."

Peep: People have apparently loved to peep since windows were invented. *Peep* is rooted in the ancient Germanic word *keek,* which, like *peep* and its relative *peek,* meant "to look through a crevice or from a place of concealment; to spy." The most famous peeper in history was Peeping Tom, who, the story goes, was the only villager to sneak a peek when Lady Godiva rode through Coventry naked. Today's *peeper* prowls around other people's windows in hopes of a peek and, if not actually struck blind like Peeping Tom, usually winds up in jail.

pay the piper at the pearly gates. But then you've also got your *venial sins* (from the Latin *venia,* "forgiveness" or "pardon")—a seemingly endless procession of smaller stuff such as fudging your taxes, filching office supplies from work, and signing your dog up for those "Ten CDs for a Buck!" offers.

It's unclear, theologically speaking, what happens to venial offenders when the final credits roll. But in the short term, at least, the pen stealers and furtive flirters have a good chance of beating the rap. One sign that you may be in the clear is if your peers refer to your crime as a *peccadillo* rather than *an outrage* or *a symptom of America in decline. Peccadillo* comes from the Spanish *peccadillo,* meaning "little sin," and since it appeared in English around 1591, *peccadillo* has been a code word for "maybe not a great idea, but nothing to get excited about." Then again, sin is subject to interpretation, and your mileage may vary in the judgment of spouses, employers, and district attorneys.

Philander

Philander is one of those words that started out with a good reputation but gradually slid, like a wayward husband in the throes of a midlife crisis, into scandal. *Philander* comes from the Greek *philandros* (a combination of *philos,* "loving," and *andros,* "man"), which meant "loving or fond of mankind," or, when applied to a woman, "loving her husband." When it first appeared in English around 1682, *philander* simply meant "ardent lover" and was used as the proper name of amorous male characters in several medieval dramas and romances, including *The Way of the World* by the great English dramatist William Congreve.

By the late eighteenth century, however, *philander* the upstanding noun had become a verb with dubious overtones. *To philander* in the eighteenth century meant "to flirt with a woman, to *make love* (when that phrase usually meant 'necking') in a trifling manner, without any serious intention of marriage."

Today the verb *philander,* and especially its agent noun *philanderer,* are words of full-blown ill repute, used almost exclusively to describe a faithless cad who habitually betrays his wife or "significant other" with tawdry affairs.

PHILANDER is one of those words that started out with a good reputation but gradually slid, like a wayward husband in the throes of a midlife crisis, into scandal.

Pine

No, not the tree. *To pine* means "to suffer a severe and persistent romantic obsession." Much as we might like pine furniture, no one in their right mind pines over the stuff, and there is no relation twixt tree and the torments of love.

The tree kind of *pine* comes from the Latin *pinus,* which is related to an earlier Indo-European word meaning "resin" or "sap," which pine trees possess in abundance. The "suffering" kind of *pine,* meaning to moon about in the wake of lost love, comes from the Latin *poena,* "punishment," which also gave us *pain* and *penalty.* When *pine* first appeared around A.D. 873, it was as a transitive verb, meaning that *to pine* meant to make someone else deeply miserable through literal torture or hardship. *Pine* eventually became largely an intransitive verb, meaning that pining is something one does to oneself, and it came to connote tortures of the mind and emotion more than physical pain. Not surprisingly, the first recorded use of this "mental torment" sense of *pine* was in Shakespeare's *Romeo and Juliet,* written around 1592.

Platonic

A disciple of Socrates, the Greek philosopher Plato held that all things are merely imperfect imitations of pure forms that exist apart from, yet can be grasped only by, the human mind. A good pizza, for instance, will never match the Platonic ideal of a pizza, which, among other attributes, always arrives hot. But it is important to strive for the Platonic ideal, so we continue to order pizza.

As an idealist, Plato was very impressed with the purity of

his teacher Socrates' love for young men, such purity being not exactly the rule in ancient Greece. Plato's ideal of pure, spiritual love (as opposed to the panting, corporeal sort) was known in Latin as *amor Platonicus.* Eventually the ideal of *platonic love* was expanded to include nonsexual love between men and women. The phrase turned up in English around 1630, and various people have been claiming to be involved in "just platonic" relationships ever since. They are, of course, almost always lying.

 Eventually the ideal of PLATONIC LOVE was expanded to include nonsexual love between men and women, and various people have been claiming to be involved in "just platonic" relationships ever since. They are, of course, almost always lying.

Pornography

Literature and art depicting sexual activity, often designed to arouse the passions of viewers and readers, have been produced by every human culture. Some of the earliest examples of erotica unearthed by archaeologists are the raunchy wall paintings adorning the orgy rooms of Roman cities, art known by the Greek term *pornographos* or "the depiction of prostitutes," a combination of *porne,*

Even in supposedly straitlaced Victorian society, pornography was hugely popular.

"prostitute" and *graphein,* "to write." English adopted the term *pornography* from the French *pornographie* around 1857, but at first it was used primarily among archaeologists to describe the racy art and literature of the ancients. By 1880, however, it was noticed that even in supposedly straitlaced Victorian society, pornography was hugely popular, and the term came to be used in reference to modern erotica as well.

Prude

Very few people today would admit to being prudes, but the word has not always carried its current derogatory overtones. *Prude* was taken directly from French, where *prude* means "a prim and proper (perhaps excessively proper) woman." The French form was based in turn on *preudefemme,* Old French for "virtuous woman" and analogous to *prudhomme,* meaning "brave or honorable man." The fragment *preu* is rooted in the Latin *prodesse,* "to do good," and is related to our modern English *proud.* So the basic meaning of *prude* was simply "good woman."

In the real world, of course, goodness and propriety are honored more in word than in deed, and *prude* today means "an uptight, disapproving, and sexually repressed scold of either sex." Pity the poor prude, who never gets invited to any really fun parties.

Puppy Love

Puppy love is the kind of innocent, idealistic infatuation often exhibited by teenagers and other simple folk—an intense attachment that often makes up for its inevitably short duration with a lifetime of bittersweet memories. But it has very little to do with dogs. In fact, before *puppy love* became a common phrase around 1834, the same phenomenon was known as *calf love,* in both cases the implication being that the affection between the parties is a product of immaturity and destined to fade as the critters grow up.

Before PUPPY LOVE became a common phrase around 1834, the same phenomenon was known as CALF LOVE.

Rendezvous

Rendezvous was borrowed by English from French, which makes it perfect for lovers seeking to add a little class or romance to their date. And on a strictly utilitarian note, a mysterious "I can't work late because I have a rendezvous" is far more likely to work on the boss than "Becky and I are going to the movies."

But while *rendezvous* retains the cachet of romance in English, the original French word denoted anything but a romantic interlude. *Rendez-vous* in French means "present yourselves" and was originally an order given to soldiers to assemble at a given place and hour. In English, *rendezvous* was originally a noun used to mean "a meeting place for soldiers" or, in non-military contexts, simply "a meeting or assembly." Today, however, the amorous overtones of the word mean that any executive describing a sales meeting as a rendezvous would probably have some explaining to do at home.

Rival

The English language seems to take delight in reminding us, every so often, that no matter how sophisticated and *evolved* we may think we are, we're still speaking the language of rural England in the days when socializing often consisted of waving to the farmer on the other side of the river.

Today a *rival* is a competitor, an adversary in pursuit of the same goal as we are, someone who seeks to grab the brass ring before we do, preferably before we're even out of bed in the morning. Modern culture has built a cult of beating out the rival in the business world, but the keenest competition in many people's lives comes on the playing fields of love and romance. Endless plays, novels, and movies have been written on the subject of romantic rivalry, and competition for the love of a desirable person is so central to human nature that even the tawdriest affair usually has at least two or three *rivals* figuratively haunting the motel parking lot. As the cellular phone ads say, it's all about choices.

So it's amusing to note, in an age when *rivals* for love spin their intrigues and maneuver for advantage in upscale bars or cappuccino parlors, that *rival* originally meant "the guy on the other side of the stream." From the Latin *rivus,* meaning "stream or river," the *rival* was a neighbor who shared a water source and possibly grazing land with you. Since neighbors naturally tend to be competitive, *rival,* which appeared in English around 1577, came to mean "someone who wants the same thing, or person, as you do."

Romance

Romance is perhaps the most complicated and fraught of all human endeavors, and our literature shows it. If all writing having at least tangentially to do with romance, marriage, affairs, affairs gone wrong, love, lost love, and love that refuses to get lost were removed from the planet Earth tomorrow, we'd probably be left with just the telephone book and the instructions for the toaster.

Even the word *romance* itself seems more complicated than it needs to be. The original meaning of *romance* when it entered English from Old French in the fourteenth century was "the language of France," specifically the French influenced by vernacular Latin (Romanicus) spoken by commoners in France (as opposed to the formal Latin of written discourse). This sense lives on in the linguistic term *Romance languages,* referring to languages rooted in the spoken Latin of the Roman Empire, such as French, Spanish, and Italian.

While Latin was still used for official documents in medieval

The original meaning of ROMANCE was "the language of France."

times, popular literature—stories about knights and dragons and the like—were published in the *romance* spoken by the rabble, and soon these "pulp fiction" stories themselves became known as *romances*. Since many of these tales centered on love and its travails, *romance* came to be associated with what we would today call a *love story*. Eventually, of course, people began to expect life to imitate these popular novels, and the modern sense of *romance* was born.

Romeo

For a stand-up guy who killed himself because he thought his first girlfriend (and wife) had died, Romeo has not fared well as a figure of speech. When *Romeo,* after the hero of Shakespeare's play, came into use as an eponym (a noun formed from a proper name) in the mid–eighteenth century, the term was synonymous with "passionate lover," "ardent paramour," and "devoted soul mate." A real catch, in other words.

Just a few short centuries later, *Romeo* has become a synonym for "womanizer," "serial seducer," and in many cases "cad." In *Romeo and Juliet,* Juliet awoke from her drugged sleep to find her lover Romeo dead, and promptly stabbed herself. Today's woman who awakes to find her Romeo gone will, at least eventually, consider herself lucky.

Salacious

Leapin' lizards! Brad Pitt and Billy Bob What's-his-name are both dating Liz Taylor! Or maybe not. But *leaping,* in the form of the Latin *salire,* "to leap," is at the root of *salacious,* which means "lustful," or "tending to provoke lust." After *salacious* first appeared in English in the seventeenth century, it was often used as a euphemism to describe the mating proclivities of animals, as in one 1774 natural history text that observed, "Animals of the hare kind . . . are remarkably salacious." This was a roundabout way of saying that bunny rabbits spend most of their time leaping on each other.

By the nineteenth century, *salacious* was more often being applied to humans leaping on each other, or thinking about leaping, or reading books that tended to encourage, in critics' eyes, illicit leaping.

Seduce

Seducere is a Latin word meaning "to lead aside or astray," and when *seduce* first appeared in English in the fifteenth century, it meant "to tempt a servant or vassal to abandon his allegiance to his master." Since such sneaky servant snatching was frowned upon among the nobility, *seduce* soon

These days, both men and women can be seduced over and over again.

took on the more general sense of "to lead a person astray; to convince someone to do wrong." This sense is still in use today, and the *seduce excuse* (for example, "The accountants said it was legal") is perennially popular among business executives and other pillars of propriety caught with their hand in the cookie jar.

But the primary sense of *seduce* is "to induce or persuade another person to engage in sexual intercourse," and has been since it appeared in the sixteenth century. While *seduction* in the sixteenth century applied primarily to the corruption of a female virgin (considered at the time to be an act of theft from the girl's parents), these days both men and women can be seduced over and over again, and the term has lost its connotation of crime.

Sex

Wouldn't you know it. Here's *the* word, the (according to some folks, including Freud) alpha and omega of human life, the big enchilada of literature, art, music, you name it, possibly the whole point of civilization (and therefore language itself), and no one is exactly certain of where it came from.

Sex, of course, can mean many things. At the most prosaic level, *sex* is the simple fact that human beings (and most other species of animal) are divided into two sorts: male and female. *Sex* can also refer to the genital differences that make that fact both apparent and functional, to the act of sexual intercourse itself (as in the strangely cold phrase *to have sex*), and to the entire issue of sexual function that infuses human life (as in the advertising-industry truism "Sex sells").

The word *sex* first appeared in English in the fourteenth century, adopted from the Old French *sexe,* which had in turn been derived from the Latin *sexus.* For many years, *sexus* was explained as a derivative of the Latin verb *secare,* meaning "to cut" and the source of such modern English words as *section* and *sector.* The reasoning behind tying *sex* to *secare* was that the human race was cut, or separated, into two genders, a theory that made perfect sense. Unfortunately, perfect sense does not make up for the lack of actual evidence for such a transformation, and the *sexus-secare* connection is now considered doubtful. So the origin of *sex* remains a mystery, which is perhaps as it should be.

Siren

You can't accuse the English language of lacking a sense of humor—not when it uses one word to mean both an alluring woman *and* an air-raid warning signal. And we're not talking *homographs*—(unrelated words that just happen to be spelled the same way, such as the archer's *bow* and the *bow* of a ship). *Siren* the beautiful woman and *siren* the wailing warning machine are the same word.

In Homer's *Odyssey,* Odysseus and his crew must sail dangerously close to the island of the Sirens, beautiful half-woman, half-bird creatures whose alluring song was said to be so hypnotic that it lured sailors to their doom on the treacherous shoals surrounding the island. To resist the Sirens' song, Odysseus has himself lashed to the mast of his ship and orders his men to stuff their ears with wax, but even then just barely makes it past the danger.

Later authors and artists made use of Homer's Sirens as symbols of lust and temptation, and the word *siren* entered English in the fourteenth century, first in the sense of the mythological creature, a sort of singing mermaid, then, more benignly, as "a woman who sings sweetly," and finally, harking back to Odysseus's ordeal, as "a woman who charms and tempts men but ultimately deceives them and leads them to ruin." This "femme fatale" sense is still in use today.

Meanwhile, in 1891, a French inventor came up with an instrument that could produce precise musical tones by interrupting a stream of water, air, or steam. The convergence of water and music prompted Charles Cagniard de La Tour to dub his invention the *siren* after Homer's singing creatures. Eventually, the principle he discovered led to the development of our modern earsplitting electric sirens.

Slut

Two interesting facts about *slut:* first, as well as being a noun meaning "a sexually loose or promiscuous woman," *slut* is also a verb meaning either "to act like a slut" or, alternatively, "to transform a woman into a slut," a sense that those in the music industry should find useful.

Second, *slut* originally had nothing to do with sex or morals. When *slut* entered modern English in the early fifteenth century from the Middle English *slutte,* it meant simply "an untidy or dirty woman," often a kitchen maid or scrubwoman. *Slut* has cousins in many European languages and may be related to a Germanic root meaning "mud puddle."

Unfairly (but perhaps inevitably), an untidy woman came to be considered probably an immoral one as well, and soon *slut* had acquired its modern meaning of "a woman of loose morals." One glimmer of justice may be dawning in the sorry saga of *slut,* however. Since the 1990s, *slut* has increasingly been applied to men as well as women.

Smut

SMUT!
Give me smut and nothing but!
A dirty novel I can't shut,
If it's uncut, and unsubt- le.

—Tom Lehrer, "Smut"

At the time Mr. Lehrer wrote his satirical song in the early 1960s, *smut* was a very serious word. Politicians campaigned against smut, J. Edgar Hoover warned against its insidious effects, and censors in Hollywood pored over movie and television scripts, hunting for the slightest hint of the dreaded smut.

As befits a word whose closest synonym long ago was

Meet Ms. Wrong

Derogatory terms for women frequently say more about male psychology than about female failings. The vocabulary of male derision falls into two general categories, roughly corresponding to the "damned if she does, damned if she doesn't" mold. On the one hand, there are terms for an unfaithful woman, that staple of country music who can't wait to "step out on" a nice, trusting guy. On the other hand, men also have several terms for women who do "stand by their man" but stand a little too close and have too many opinions.

Bitch and *slut* are probably the most common epithets applied to women today. *Bitch,* meaning literally "female dog," entered English around A.D. 1000 and by 1400 was being applied to women. Interestingly, *bitch* originally described a loose or immoral woman, but in modern use it is usually applied to a woman who is difficult or excessively critical. This modern sense has also made *bitch* a verb meaning "to criticize harshly," and in a dubious sign of progress, men can now be said to *bitch.*

Unfortunately (from a linguistic viewpoint at least) the popular dependence on *bitch* and *slut* has obscured a number of now-antiquated (but still heard) epithets that describe a more nuanced spectrum of female behavior.

Chippy: From the nineteenth century, slang for a woman of easy virtue (but not necessarily a prostitute) of the sort that frequented low bars and dives. *Chippy* was originally a nineteenth-century term for a sparrow or any small bird given to constant chirping, to which the giggles and frivolity of the human chippy were likened.

Tramp: *To tramp* originally meant "to walk" and gave us the male *tramp,* a hobo or vagrant who wanders without home or job. A female *tramp* wanders from man to man. While the male *tramp* first appeared in English in the seventeenth century, the promiscuous female *tramp* didn't appear in our language until the 1920s.

Hussy: Often preceded by *brazen,* the combination meaning "a loud or rude loose woman," hussy started out in the sixteenth century as simply a variation of *housewife.* As in the case of *slut,* which originally meant "an untidy woman," such as a kitchen maid, *hussy's* lower-class connotation eventually took on overtones of "promiscuous" or "immoral."

Floozy: A loose, lower-class young woman, often cheaply flashy; a bimbo. Also spelled *floosie, floozie,* and *floogy,* the term *floozy* appeared around 1920 and was popularized by the 1938 hit song "Flat Foot Floogie" by Slim Gaillard. The origin of *floozy* is uncertain, but it may be connected to the old dialect term *floosy,* meaning "fluffy" or "soft."

Minx: *Minx* has nothing to do with the mink coat dangled as a lure by the rich sugar daddy. Perhaps an altered form of the Dutch *minneken,* meaning "sweetheart" or "beloved," *minx* first appeared in English in the sixteenth century as a popular name for pet dogs. But it was almost immediately also used to mean "a bold, flirtatious young woman," the sense that survives today. Like *vixen, minx* is a malleable term. To be labeled a *minx* by a man is usually a compliment, but applied by one woman to another, *minx* is an insult.

Meet Ms. Wrong continued

Jezebel: Jezebel was the wife of King Ahab in the Old Testament, and as wives go she was a pretty serious disaster. A worshipper of Baal, Jezebel painted herself with gaudy makeup, flaunted her beauty and wantonness, and brought evil upon the kingdom of Israel. Eventually Jezebel went too far and was tossed from a window and devoured by dogs. Since the sixteenth century, *Jezebel* has meant "an immoral, conniving woman."

Vixen: The *vixen* is the female fox, known for its ferocity in defending its cubs. *Vixen* first appeared in English in the "fox" sense in the fifteenth century, and by the sixteenth century it was being applied to human females considered argumentative or quarrelsome. But *vixen* differs from *bitch* in that men may consider a *vixen* spicy or challenging, while a *bitch* is always bad news.

Shrew: Another animal term, this time a small, mouselike creature, reputed in folktales to have evil powers. Originally applied to wicked and devious men, a *shrew* is now a woman who constantly scolds and nags.

Virago: *Virago* was not originally an insult. From *vir*, Latin for "man," in the fourteenth century a *virago* was a heroic woman or woman warrior. Unfortunately, this sense is now rarely heard, and *virago* has become synonymous with "bad-tempered bitch."

Harpy: In Greek and Roman mythology, the *harpy* was a fearsome creature with the body of a woman but the wings and talons of a hawk and was often dispatched by the gods to wreak divine vengeance by plucking its victims to pieces. In a figurative sense, *harpy* has been used since the sixteenth century to mean "a rapacious, greedy woman."

"dirty," *smut* is derived from the Middle High German *smutzen,* meaning "to make dirty; to blacken." When *smut* first appeared in English in the fourteenth century as *smotten,* it meant "to smudge or mark with some dirty substance," a sense still found in the agricultural definition of *smut,* meaning "a black fungus that ruins crops." *Smut* in the sense of "indecent or obscene language or pictures" first appeared toward the end of the seventeenth century. Today, *smut* has largely been replaced in the popular vocabulary by *pornography.*

Spoon

Though rarely heard today, until the mid–twentieth century *spoon* was a popular term for the sort of behavior that now goes by the broader and far less enchanted terms *flirting* and *fooling around.*

Though spoons in the flatware sense do not usually play a role in spooning, there is an interesting, if somewhat oblique, connection between the terms. *Spoon* as an eating utensil derives from the Old English *spon,* which meant "chip of wood." Pretty early on, folks discovered that a chip or sliver of wood with a slightly concave surface could be used to convey liquids, such as soup, from bowl to mouth, and the modern dining sense of *spoon* appeared around A.D. 1340.

Over the next several centuries, *spoon* sprouted a wide range of related and sometimes figurative meanings, including *born with a silver spoon in his mouth,* meaning "born to a life of privilege." *To spoon* from the nineteenth century on has also

By the early nineteenth century, a young man in love with a young woman was said to be SPOONS about her.

meant "to cuddle or sleep next to someone, back-to-front," like spoons nestled in a drawer.

In the late eighteenth century, *spoon* was used as slang for "a simpleton" or "a shallow, foolish person," probably in joking reference to the shallow concave shape of a real spoon. Silly or foolish behavior was termed *spoony*, and by the early nineteenth century a young man in love with a young woman was said to be *spoons* about her. Within a few years, by 1831, *spooning* had come to mean "courting, especially in an excessively sentimental or effusive fashion."

Spouse

Of all the terms for a partner in marriage, *spouse* is probably the most neutral and drab, at least partly because it is not gender-specific and thus can be applied to both men and women. This makes *spouse* ideal for use on census forms and credit applications. Yet at the root of *spouse* is the solemn promise that marriage embodies, and your *spouse* is the person to whom you are bound by the promises made during the wedding ceremony. The Latin verb *spondere* meant "to promise; to bind oneself to," from which also developed our modern English words *espouse* (originally "to promise to marry") and *sponsor* (meaning "to promise to support").

String Along

Hope springs eternal, especially among the hopeless. The gullible mistress who waits years for her married lover to divorce his wife, or the "nice guy" who brings flowers to a hooker, persist in their devotions against all reason, almost as if they were physically tied to their folly. *String along* has been slang for "to lead someone on by encouraging misplaced confidence" since at least 1902 and probably comes from the circa 1812 British slang *to string,* meaning "to deceive." An equivalent term from the nineteenth century was *to get* (or *take*) *in tow.*

Stud

There was a time when a stud would have been expected to emit an odor—a strong, horsy odor. The original meaning of *stud,* when it entered Old English from the Germanic root *sto,* was "a place where horses are bred." (The root *sto* also gave us the English words *stall, steed,* and, since horses spend a lot of time on their feet, *stand.*)

Fairly quickly, *stud* came to be used to mean "a group of horses owned and bred by one person," and by the nineteenth century, *stud* was usually applied to a stallion

There was a time when a stud would have been expected to emit an odor—a strong horsy odor.

or other male animal kept exclusively for breeding. *Stud* as slang for a certain breed of human behavior was not far behind, and by the late nineteenth century, *stud* had become popular slang for "a serial seducer or womanizer, a man of great sexual prowess or success."

Sugar Daddy

A *sugar daddy* is an older, often elderly, man who provides financial support to a much younger woman, almost always in exchange for (or at least in expectation of) a sexual relationship. *Sugar daddy* has been popular slang since at least the 1920s, but any hope of a chaste one-way relationship with a sugar daddy evaporates after a look at the roots of the term. As long ago as 1681, daddy was common slang among prostitutes for an older man, and in the early twentieth century a hooker's *daddy* was her boyfriend-pimp. And lest there be any lingering doubts as to the basis for this kind of relationship, the *sugar* in *sugar daddy* has been slang for "money" since the mid–nineteenth century.

The SUGAR in SUGAR DADDY
has been slang for "money" since
the mid—nineteenth century.

Suitor

You think that you are Ann's suitor; that you are
the pursuer and she the pursued; that it is your
part to woo, to persuade, to prevail, to overcome.
Fool: it is you who are the pursued, the marked
down quarry, the destined prey.

—George Bernard Shaw, *Man and Superman*

For an enterprise that is generally thought to require the enthusiasm of both partners, love certainly seems to involve a lot of chasing. The "pursued"? The "quarry"? The "destined prey"? Perhaps it is not mere coincidence that the marriage rate has fallen in recent decades while sales of running shoes have zoomed.

The modern *suitor* is gender-specific: a *suitor* is a man seeking a given woman's hand in marriage, but no such term exists for a woman who has her sights set on a particular man. The original definition of *suitor,* in keeping with the ever popular chase metaphor, is "one who follows." The Vulgar Latin *sequere* (variant of Latin *sequi,* "to follow") begot a raft of modern English words, including *sect* (for "a group of followers"), *suite* ("a group of related objects," and essentially the same word as *suit*), and *sue,* which now means "to pursue through legal action." A *suitor,* when the word first appeared in English in the thirteenth century, was originally simply a loyal follower or attendant at the royal court of a monarch. By the early sixteenth century, *suitor* had acquired the meaning of "a petitioner or plaintiff in a suit" and, more important, "one who seeks earnestly." By the late sixteenth century, *suitor* had arrived at its modern meaning, and the chase was on.

Swain

Swain arrived in English in the twelfth century from the Old Norse *sveinn* and at first meant simply "boy" or "servant," particularly a young man serving a knight.

By the sixteenth century, knights were getting scarce, and *swain* took on the meaning of "farm boy." Since the country life was considered a simpler, purer existence, poets began to use *swain* in the sense of "gallant lover" in their pastoral fantasies. Five centuries later, we still use *swain,* but almost always in a jocular or sarcastic tone, as in "Deborah's swain turned out to be a mousy accountant with a wife in Hoboken."

Deborah's swain turned out to be a mousy accountant with a wife in Hoboken.

Sweetheart

Sweet has been used as an adjective to mean "beloved" since at least the fourteenth century, and *heart* has, since the same period, been synonymous with "lover" (although it's difficult to imagine anyone today saying, "Pick me up a six-pack at the supermarket, will you, heart?"). But until the eighteenth century, the two were almost always treated by writers as separate words or hyphenated as *sweet-heart*. Today, *sweetheart* is solidly one word and, along with *darling, honey,* and *dear,* is spoken by millions of couples every day.

Sweetheart as an affectionate form of address is a bit more neutral than it has been in the past and is thus more flexible than the common alternatives, such as *darling* (which implies passion) or *baby* (which implies a motorcycle in the vicinity). Mothers, for instance, often address their children as *sweetheart*.

Swoon

Not many people seem to swoon in real life anymore, though judging from classic movies, swooning was quite common even as recently as the 1940s. Nearly any woman on screen was likely to swoon when confronted with a stressful situation, whether it was a breakup with her beau or abduction by King Kong. Inevitably, a look of shock would cross the damsel's face, a soft cry would escape her lips, and she would collapse into the arms of either a conveniently attentive swain or a giant gorilla, depending on the movie. Male characters in movies only swooned when they won enormous sums of money. Swooning in old movies was an emotional exclamation point, a theatrical signal to the audience that something really important had just happened. Swooning in the movies was dramatic.

So it may come as a bit of a letdown to learn that swooning is really just plain old fainting, as likely to be caused by low blood sugar as by the loss of one's plantation to those dastardly Yankees. *Swoon* appeared in the late thirteenth century, meaning "to have a fainting fit; to faint," derived from the thoroughly unromantic Old English *geswogen,* related to *aswogan,* which meant "to choke."

Judging from classic movies, swooning was quite common even as recently as the 1940s.

Sybarite

Once upon a time, long, long ago (700 B.C., to be precise), the ancient Greeks founded a colony called Sybaris near the present-day city of Terranova di Sibari in southern Italy. The inhabitants of Sybaris, known as *Sybarites,* were very fortunate. Their land was extraordinarily fertile, and their location by the sea brought them lucrative trade. Living was easy in Sybaris, and over time the Sybarites became famous all over the ancient world for their devotion to pleasure, luxury, and the frivolous. The Sybarites, it was said, even taught their horses to dance to music played on pipes.

But no one likes a slacker, and after a few hundred years of enduring the raucous giggling coming from Sybaris, their neighbors in the less prosperous city of Croton were royally fed up. According to legend, in 510 B.C. the Crotons sneaked into Sybaris bearing their own pipes and played them while attacking the city's defenders, whereupon the Sybarites' horses, instead of charging the invaders, broke into lively jigs. The victorious Crotons destroyed Sybaris and, after the Sybarites had painstakingly rebuilt their city and started giggling again, came back and destroyed it again in 457 B.C.

But while the silly giggling of Sybaris may forever be stilled, *sybarite* has come to mean "one who is devoted to personal pleasure, especially the pleasures of love and sex, over all else."

Tryst

The *New Fowler's Modern English Usage* calls *tryst* an "archaic word for a date, an assignation," but we beg to differ. *Tryst*, in addition to being a staple of the popular romance novel, is alive and well in nearly every issue of nearly every supermarket tabloid in America. Movie stars, after all, do not go on dates. People who live in Des Moines go on dates; movie stars have trysts.

The great thing about *tryst*, from a tabloid editor's viewpoint, is its brevity compared to the alternatives *rendezvous* (which usually lacks the seaminess of *tryst*) and *assignation* (which readers may not understand anyway). The same economy accounts for the popularity of such terms as *hooker, brawl, shocker, gal pal, spat,* and the inevitable *dumped* on tabloid front pages.

Tryst first appeared in English around 1375, adopted from the Old French word *tristre,* meaning "an appointed station in hunting" (that is, a spot where a hunter was supposed to stand as other hunters drove the game toward him). Over the past few centuries, *tryst* has gone from meaning simply "a prearranged meeting" to being used almost exclusively to mean "a secret meeting of lovers."

Two-Timer

Modern life is a ballet of doing two things at once. We set the coffee to brewing as we head for our morning shower. We listen to books on tape as we commute. We type E-mail as we field phone calls from the boss. And we let Mr. Microwave play chef as we watch the evening news.

So it's a bit ironic that what is possibly the oldest kind of multitasking—*two-timing,* or carrying on a romantic relationship with two (or more) people at once, each of whom believes that he or she is the sole object of affection—while no doubt efficient, from the practitioner's viewpoint, is nearly universally condemned.

Two-time first appeared as slang in the United States in the early 1920s, probably as simply a shortened form of *two at a time.*

Unrequited

Love is *unrequited* when only one person (as opposed to the optimal two) is interested in a relationship and has had his or her amorous advances greeted by indifference at best and laughter at worst. The unrequited one then either gets on with life or, more likely, becomes a tear-soaked stalker and the pity of his or her friends.

Unrequited love has been a perennial subject of art and literature since art and literature consisted of cave paintings. But at the root of *unrequited* is an even older human sentiment: "You owe me."

To requite means simply "to repay" or "to return in kind." Such consideration is simply good manners. If we were to bake you a cake on your birthday, for example, it is likely that our own birthday would dawn to find us tapping our feet and wondering whether said gesture would be requited. So a smitten gallant who proffers his heart to a fair maiden will likely do so in the expectation that his gift of love will be requited.

Requite, which first appeared in English in the early sixteenth century, is based on the verb *to quite,* an antiquated form of the

Looking for Mister Won't-Hit-on-My-Sister

Finding Mr. Right would be a lot easier if the playing fields of love and dating weren't so full of Mr. Wrongs. Exact figures are hard to come by, but many single women would estimate that somewhere between 75 percent and 110 percent of eligible men, once closely examined, turn out to be ineligible owing to flaws ranging from poor personal hygiene to already being married to someone else. The sad state of the male side of the gene pool is, alas, nothing new, and history has supplied a range of terms for the boyfriend from hell. Here are a few, in ascending order of odiousness.

Rogue: Although it meant "vagrant" or "tramp" when it appeared in the sixteenth century, *rogue* today is a mild word for a mischievous womanizer. Often heard in the phrase *charming rogue,* indicating that no one takes the rogue's shenanigans very seriously.

Jerk: The default category for a misbehaving boyfriend. A *jerk* usually hasn't done anything truly awful but makes up for it by being, in retrospect, utterly without redeeming qualities. *Jerk* appeared in the 1930s and is thought to be short for *jerk-off,* an eighteenth-century insult meaning "habitual masturbator."

Rat: Probably not fair to real rats, but it has been used as slang for a sneaky, dishonest, and disloyal person since at least the fifteenth century. A *rat* is a jerk you're still mad at.

Heel: The dirtball who runs off with your roommate the day after you send out the wedding invitations. Appeared in the early twentieth century as criminal slang for a double-crosser. Why *heel?* Probably because you can't get any lower.

Cad: A career heel who makes a habit of deceiving women. Short for *caddie,* originally slang for a lower-class errand boy in the nineteenth century.

Bounder: A nineteenth-century British term for a man whose perfidy transcends all limits or bounds of decency and morals. The lowlife who comes to meet your parents and leaves with your little sister *and* your father's credit cards is a *bounder.*

Creep: Originally short for *creeper,* nineteenth-century slang for a shifty person who sneaks around, up to no good. Fortunately, most women can recognize a creep at a distance, but many end up working for creepy bosses.

Pig: Again, not fair to the animal, but *pig* has meant "a selfish person" since the fifteenth century. Today's male *pig* is a shortening of *male chauvinist pig,* a 1960s term for a man who contemptuously treats women as objects.

verb *to quit* used in an equally antiquated sense meaning "to repay, to give back." *Unrequited love* is, etymologically speaking anyway, "love that has been given and not repaid."

Valentine

Traditionalists call February 14 *Saint Valentine's Day,* but there are actually several saints by that name. The two most famous Saint Valentines, both martyrs of the early Christian church, met their deaths on the same day only a few years apart. That day was not, however, February 14, which was simply the "name day" of everyone named Valentine. There isn't even any special connection between either of the Saint Valentines and lovers. Ancient cultures celebrated the period of mid-February as the mating time of birds, and young people in the Roman Empire chose sweethearts for the coming year by picking names from a basket. By the late eighteenth century, Saint Valentine's Day had become the occasion for lovers to exchange gifts and cards, which eventually led to a bonanza for the modern greeting-card industry. Today it is left to the cynics among us to remember that Saint Valentine's Day was, from the beginning, for the birds.

Today it is left to the cynics among us to remember that Saint Valentine's Day was, from the beginning, for the birds.

Vamp

Vamp is a strange little word with several senses. To a shoemaker, a *vamp* is the part of a shoe or boot that covers the portion of the foot in front of the ankle. *Vamp* in this sense is a short form of the French *avant pied,* meaning literally "before the foot." *Vamp* is also found in the verb *to vamp,* originally a shoemaker's term meaning "to repair" (as by replacing the vamp of a shoe), now mostly heard in the form *revamp,* meaning "to modify something so as to make it work better."

Vamp is also used at various places in the United States as slang for "a volunteer firefighter," a usage that appears to be unrelated to the "shoe" sense, although its origins are unknown.

But a far more intriguing sense of *vamp* arose in the early twentieth century, when *vamp* (in this case short for *vampire*) came into use as slang for "a predatory breed of woman who attracts, exploits, and then discards men." The most famous *vamp* was probably the silent-screen actress Theda Bara, who gained notoriety and popularized the vamp with her 1915 performance in the film *A Fool There Was,* adapted from a Rudyard Kipling poem titled "The Vampire."

> The most famous VAMP was probably the silent-screen actress Theda Bara.

Virgin

Oddly enough, for a term that connotes purity and innocence, *virgin* has been a taboo word for much of its life. Derived from the Latin *virgo,* "maiden," via the French *virgine, virgin* was a religious term when it appeared in English in the thirteenth century, meaning "a devout and unmarried woman." In general use since the fifteenth century, *virgin* has meant "a person, especially a girl or a woman, who has never had sexual intercourse." But on the apparent principle that the sober negative raises the possibility of the scandalous positive, *virgin* was, until the mid–twentieth century, considered unfit for polite conversation and indecent in books, movies, and drama. According to Hugh Rawson in his book *Wicked Words,* it wasn't until producer Otto Preminger sued several censorship boards over their banning of his film *The Moon Is Blue* in 1953 that filmgoers were allowed to hear such racy terms as *virgin* and *seduce.*

Wed

Till death do us part, unless we roll snake eyes. Anyone who has ever attended a wedding and later cynically speculated on the statistically dicey odds of the matrimonial union's being permanent has some surprising support in the history of the word *wed* itself. The root of *wed* is the Germanic *wathjam,* which meant "pledge" or "promise." So a *wedding* is a ceremony where a bride and groom solemnly promise each other to love, honor, and so on. But that Germanic root is also the source of other English words, among them *wage* (a promise to pay), *engage* (to promise to do something), and, uh-oh, *wager,* as in "gambling bet." As a matter of fact, one of the earliest meanings of *wed* in fourteenth-century English was "to wager or bet something," as in "You wed your life." The "wager" sense of *wed* is now said to be obsolete, but that fact probably hasn't improved anyone's odds.

On the apparent principle that the sober negative raises the possibility of the scandalous positive, virgin was, until the mid—twentieth century, considered unfit for polite conversation.

Whoopee, Making

For a species that has developed remarkably sophisticated languages, human beings still rely on, and utter every day, some pretty primal noises. *Ugh, ouch, yikes, whee, yay, hooray, hi,* and their relatives may be the most common words actually spoken by English speakers, yet none of these interjections actually "means" anything—they

People have probably been whooping it up since the first cave cocktail party, but WHOOP is first found in print in English in the sixteenth century.

arose as spontaneous noises made by humans in moments of excitement, joy, or distress. (Linguists call them *onomatopoeic* or *echoic* formations.)

Whoop is both an expression of excitement and a word meaning the sound itself (as in "whoops of joy"). People have probably been whooping it up since the first cave cocktail party, but *whoop* is first found in print in English in the sixteenth century. By the eighteenth century, *whoop* had spawned the even more exuberant *whoopee,* which, in the 1920s, also became a slang term meaning "lively revelry" or "rowdy behavior." *Making whoopee,* popularized in 1928 by the Donaldson and Kahn song and musical "Making Whoopee," was coined as a double entendre for both general high-spirited behavior and sexual activity.

Wife

There was a time when simply being born female and living past puberty was a 100 percent guarantee that you would someday become a wife. No, there was no Universal Marriage Act, no national lottery matching up mobs of Mr. and Ms. Rights, no mass weddings in the local stadium. It was all in the definition of *wife.*

When *wife* first appeared in English around A.D. 725, inherited from the Old English *wif*, it simply meant "woman." Thus any woman past puberty was considered a wife. The word *wife* was also, during the same period, used to mean "married woman," but it took a few centuries for that to become the predominate meaning of *wife*. And even after the change in meaning took hold, a range of terms reflecting the older sense of *wife* as "woman" remained in use, including the now-antiquated *fishwife* (meaning "female fish seller") and *alewife* (meaning "barmaid"), as well as the still-current *midwife*.

Meanwhile, the Old English *wif* had spawned another useful word. Combined with the Old English *man* (precursor of our modern *man*), *wif* produced *wifman* (literally "woman-man"), which by the thirteenth century, through a process of phonetic change that replaced the *wif* with *wo*, became our modern word *woman*. The presence of *man* in our word *woman* has greatly annoyed some modern feminists, who have devised alternatives such as *womyn*, but public acceptance of these alternatives has been very limited.

Wolf

If Little Red Riding Hood had read her Chaucer, she'd have hit the road right away and never have taken time to wonder about her grandmother's unusually big teeth. The wolf (also known as *Canis lupus*) has been used as a symbol of ferocious cruelty since at least A.D. 900, and Shakespeare frequently invoked the wolf to describe

Wolving is still considered largely a male disorder.

the darker side of human nature, as in *Julius Caesar*: "And why should Caesar be a tyrant then? Poor man! I know he would not be a wolf but that he sees the Romans are but sheep."

By the early eighteenth century, *wolf* and its verb form, *to wolve,* were being used to describe lustful, sexually predatory men, and the modern human wolf has been prowling ever since. Although *wolf* has occasionally been applied to sexually aggressive women (sometimes in the awkward form *wolfess*), wolving is still considered largely a male disorder.

Woo

Come, woo me, woo me; for now I am in a holiday humor, and like enough to consent.

—William Shakespeare, *As You Like It*

We call it *pitching woo* when one person romances another, and we've been calling it that since the eleventh century. Of course, folks must have been wooing each other long before the word came along, or we'd never have gotten as far as the eleventh century in the first place. But why *woo*? It is possible that *woo,* like many English words, arose as the imitation of sounds associated with the action, in this case the soft murmuring of lovers.

EVAN MORRIS

Yearn

Acynic might suspect that the word *yearn,* meaning "to long for; to have a strong desire for," has remained popular at least in part because *yearning* rhymes so well with *burning* in both the lyrics of great love songs (including the Cole Porter classic "Night and Day") and ream upon ream of bad poetry.

But the human penchant for yearning after what we lack, whether it be love, freedom, a particular brand of car, or eternal life, has been a hallmark of our species since long before *yearn* first appeared in thirteenth-century English.

The word *yearn* sounds so much like the feeling of emptiness and longing it describes that it might have developed from the anguished cry of a forlorn lover. Among the secondary meanings of *yearn,* in fact, are "to cry like a hound" and "to give a sound suggesting strong desire," presumably the sort of strangled moan emitted by a spurned paramour.

In fact, *yearn* developed from Germanic roots meaning "to be eager" or "to desire," none of which sounded anything like a cry of love.

Unfortunately, the Old English root of *yearn,* the awkward *geornan,* shoots down that romantic theory, as it sounds more like a brand of beer than a cry of love. Still, the fact that all of *yearn*'s ancestors, dating all the way back to its ancient Germanic roots, signified the same "can't live without you" feeling must mean something, even if only that human beings always want most what they cannot have.

Yen

First, let's explain the "money" kind of *yen*. Although the yen has been, since 1871, the official currency of Japan, the word itself comes from the Chinese word *yuan,* meaning "round thing" or "dollar."

Now, much as we all might yen for dollars or Japanese yen, the "desire" sense of *yen* comes from a far more powerful addiction: opium. The Chinese (Cantonese, to be specific) word for "opium" is *yin* or *in* (Chinese words are notoriously difficult to render in English, which accounts for the ambiguity). The word *yan* meant "craving," and the victim of *in-yan* was someone afflicted with an insatiable appetite for the drug, an opium addict.

Now, much as we all might yen for dollars or Japanese yen, the "desire" sense of YEN comes from a far more powerful addiction: opium.

With the influx of Chinese laborers into the United States during the nineteenth century, the slang term *in-yan* entered English as *yen-yen,* meaning "craving for opium," and eventually one of the *yen* was dropped, leaving us, by about 1876, with just *yen.*

Perhaps the most remarkable part of the story of *yen* is how the word has changed since it arrived in our language. Originally referring to one of the most tenacious and destructive forms of drug addiction, by about 1906 *yen* had softened to the point of meaning a sort of dreamy yearning for something or someone. Stella Gibbons used the term in this whimsical sense in her novel *Cold Comfort Farm* in 1932: "Ezra, who had a secret yen for horticulture."

So the next time your friend announces that she has a yen for Mel Gibson, just be thankful that the word *yen* isn't quite what it used to be.

BIBLIOGRAPHY

In writing this book I have had the advantage of both a large personal collection of reference works and access to electronic references on the Internet. More often than not, however, I have found myself returning to the short list of works listed below.

The sine qua non in the field of English language etymology is *The Oxford English Dictionary,* 2nd ed. (Oxford: Oxford University Press, 1989), which currently is available in four forms: the twenty-volume full edition, the single-volume compact edition (which uses microscopic type to squeeze nine pages of the full edition onto each page and comes with a very nice magnifier), a CD-ROM edition, and the *OED Online* (by subscription, at www.oed.com). Many public libraries also offer free access to one or more versions of the *OED*.

Other reference works that I have found especially useful include:

Ammer, Christine. *Have a Nice Day—No Problem! A Dictionary of Clichés.* New York: Penguin Books USA, 1992.

Ayto, John. *Twentieth Century Words.* Oxford: Oxford University Press, 1999.

———. *Dictionary of Word Origins.* New York: Little, Brown and Company, 1991.

Barnhart, Robert K. *The Barnhart Concise Dictionary of Etymology.* New York: HarperCollins Publishers, 1995.

Chapman, Robert L. *Dictionary of American Slang.* 3rd ed. New York: HarperCollins Publishers, 1995.

Dalzell, Tom. *Flappers 2 Rappers: American Youth Slang.* Springfield, MA: Merriam-Webster, Inc., 1996.

Dibbley, Dale Corey. *From Achilles' Heel to Zeus's Shield: A Lively, Informative Guide to More Than 300 Words and Phrases Born of Mythology.* New York: Fawcett Columbine, 1993.

Dickson, Paul. *Slang.* New York: Simon and Schuster Inc., 1998.

Green, Jonathan. *Slang down the Ages.* London: Kyle Cathie Limited, 1993.

Hendrickson, Robert. *The Dictionary of Eponyms: Names That Became Words.* Briarcliff Manor, NJ: Stein and Day, 1972.

Lighter, J. E. (ed). *Random House Historical Dictionary of American Slang,* 2 vols. New York: Random House, 1994 and 1997 (further volumes in progress).

Morris, William, and Mary D. Morris. *Dictionary of Word and Phrase Origins.* 2nd ed. New York: HarperCollins Publishers, 1988.

Partridge, Eric. *Dictionary of Slang and Unconventional English.* 8th ed. New York: Macmillan Publishing Company, 1984.

Rawson, Hugh. *Devious Derivations.* New York: Crown Publishers Inc., 1994.

———. Rawson's *Dictionary of Euphemisms and Other Double-talk.* New York: Crown Publishers, Inc., 1995.

———. *Wicked Words.* New York: Crown Publishers, Inc, 1989.

Room, Adrian. *Dunces, Gourmands and Petticoats: 1,300 Words Whose Meanings Have Changed through the Ages.* Chicago: NTC Publishing Group, 1997.

Wells, Diana. *100 Flowers and How They Got Their Names.* Chapel Hill, NC: Algonquin Books of Chapel Hill, 1997.

WEB SITES

Aside from my own Word Detective Web site (**www.word-detective.com**), there are an ever-increasing number of Web sites devoted to words and language. Here are some of the excellent sites I have found helpful in researching this book:

American Dialect Society (www.americandialect.org). The ADS is a scholarly organization studying the English language in North America, and produces the journal *American Speech.* On the ADS Web site, you can read back issues of the ADS newsletter, subscribe to the ADS-L E-mail discussion list, search the ADS-L archives, and, of course, join the ADS.

Bartleby.com (www.bartleby.com). An extraordinarily useful, free on-line library of classic fiction, nonfiction, reference works, and verse, all searchable.

World Wide Words (www.quinion.com/words). A fascinating word and phrase origin site from the U.K., regularly updated.

Word Play (www.wolinskyweb.com/word.htm). A site offering dozens of links to other sites that feature "fun with words." Judi Wolinsky, the author of this page, has done an excellent job of assembling these links and updates her list frequently.

BIBLIOGRAPHY